TREASURY OF
GREEK
MYTHOLOGY

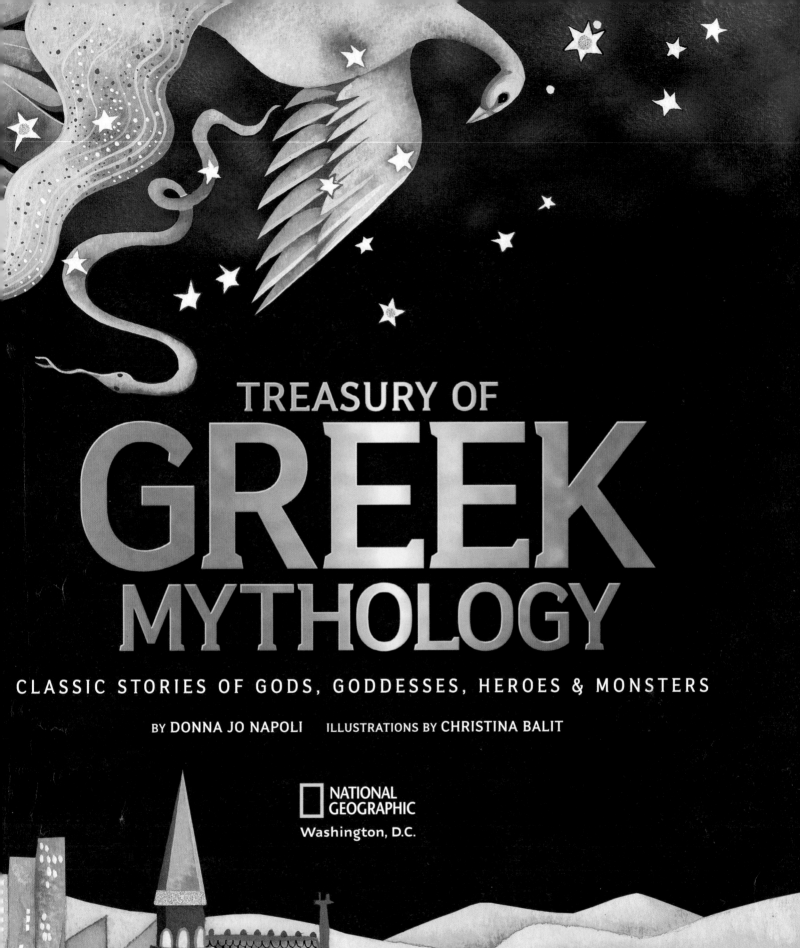

TREASURY OF
GREEK
MYTHOLOGY

CLASSIC STORIES OF GODS, GODDESSES, HEROES & MONSTERS

BY **DONNA JO NAPOLI**   ILLUSTRATIONS BY **CHRISTINA BALIT**

**NATIONAL
GEOGRAPHIC**

Washington, D.C.

TABLE OF CONTENTS

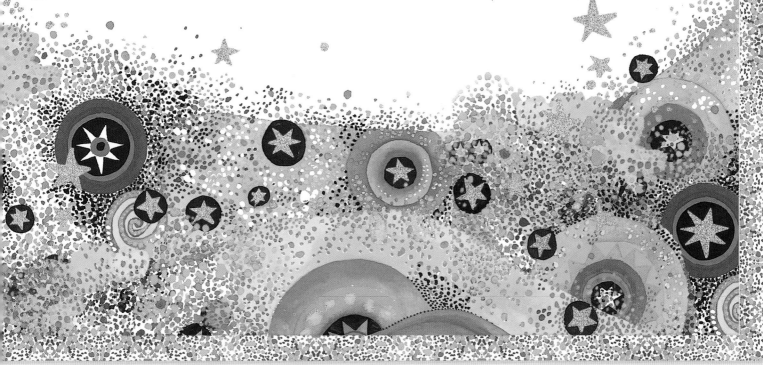

Some things about daily life can be counted on. The sun rises, crosses the sky, sets. Stars come out at night. Rivers flow toward the sea. The air and land and waters burst with life. These life-forms feed one another: Plants are eaten by animals, which are eaten by other animals. But there are also interruptions: volcanoes, earthquakes, tsunamis, storms. Life on Earth is complex.

From our earliest records of human activity, we can conclude that people recognized this complexity and wanted to explain it. So far as we know, humans are the only creatures who entertain a wide variety of questions about the nature of existence. The questions that people from different societies raise are often quite similar, but the answers they give and the relative importance they assign to these answers

can be significantly different. And those answers define the human values of our societies. They are at once based on intellect, experience, and emotion. And from them, we draw our ethics, our rituals, and our storytelling.

In this book we find answers offered by the ancient Greeks to many of the questions humans long to understand. But we also find gods, goddesses, heroes, and monsters who love and hate and grow jealous and get duped; they are blessed and cursed with all the emotions that enrich and plague ordinary humans. In reading the myths, we begin to understand that the ancient Greeks must have wanted more than just the big answers from their gods. They must have also wanted their gods to be a reflection that could help them understand themselves.

From the earliest nothingness came air and water and earth, all churning and whirling until they were inextricably bound and life became inevitable: A tree sprouted and grew strong and unruly, fruited with gods and goddesses whose powers thrived under the sun and moon and stars, stretching into every corner of the universe. That tree would nourish and confound the lives of the simple mortals yet to come.

OLYMPUS FAMILY TREE

GAIA
Mother Earth

How do you get something from nothing? Not easily, it would seem.

From empty Chaos, somehow sea and earth and air appeared. They drifted around, pieces of each getting lost in the other. No water was swimmable, no land was walkable, no gas was breathable. Anything hot could quickly turn cold. Anything cold could burst into flames. Shapes shifted, textures shifted. Objects merged one into the other effortlessly, then suddenly—slam! One or both turned inexplicably hard. What was heavy became weightless. What was weightless crashed through earth and sea and air, shattering and splattering and scattering bits of everything and nothing.

Rules of nature? They didn't operate. Indeed, there was no nature. There was nothing reliable in this turmoil except lack of order. And lack is the essence of need.

Out of that original need came the mother force, Gaia. All on her own. Need can do that.

Gaia sucked up heat and stored it in her heart. She wrapped herself round and round with anything solid she could reach, growing firmer with each layering. She pulled together her glassy sands, lifting them, grain by grain—free of air, to form deserts; free of water, to form beaches. She pushed together gigantic plates of rock until her mountains rose high, so far from

> Gaia is the flowing circle of heat, whose energy allowed land and sea and air to gather and welcome life. She's known as Mother Earth.

her scalding heart that snow settled on their peaks.

As Gaia disentangled herself from the waters and the gases, the seas fell together in giant puddles, the heavens arched over it all. In this way the emergence of Gaia led to both the wholeness of the seas, called Pontus, and the wholeness of the heavens, called Uranus.

But Gaia was generous, as a mother should be. She opened her veins so water could rush through rivers and creeks, and pool together in large low lakes and small hidden ponds. She yielded here and there to the gases, allowing crevices to cradle them. One in particular was huge and gaping: the waiting hole for the dead. But at this point she didn't know that. She knew things only as they happened, like a child encountering everything for the first time. She created the hole almost as though she understood instinctually all the gain and loss that would follow from her generosity.

The seas learned from Gaia and welcomed islands. The skies learned from Gaia and welcomed stars. And then the seas and skies went further and worked together to cycle water from the salty seas to the skies, then fresh and sweet to the lands, who returned it once more to the seas.

But Gaia was not the only child of the enormous original need; there were two others. One was Tartarus, the Underworld. The other was Eros, the god of love. Then

Chaos gave a giant yawn and out flowed the total darkness of Night as well as Erebus. Erebus, like Gaia, was a place as well as a force, seeking to fill crannies. Erebus settled into the hole for the dead and became the upper part of the Underworld.

Eros was beautiful, but not ordinary beautiful. Eros' beauty made the others quiver. It made them dream of being enveloped in warm caresses. Of getting drunk on thick creamy honey. Of swooning from ambrosia. Of whirling to tinkling music. Of being dazzled by sparkles in this lightless world.

So Night and Erebus fell in love, and Night gave birth to Day. And with light, in the lushness of fresh and salty water and in the expansiveness of air, life on Earth began. Grasses and vines wound their way around the globe. Bushes gently bloomed.

Gaia watched Night and Erebus with envy. She felt so alone. She was the cause of all this wonder, yet none of it satisfied her. She was hungry, longing, needy. And so she turned to the heavens and the seas—Uranus and Pontus. She loved them both, of course. But Uranus seemed soothing, while Pontus seemed raging. So she chose Uranus as her husband.

Let There Be LIGHT

Around the world, stories of the creation of life appear. Usually the sun plays an important role in these stories, which is no surprise, given how important the sun is to life on Earth. Greek mythology is different in a strange way, though: Daylight appears early in the creation story, but daylight is not connected to the sun, at least not initially. Interestingly, in the Book of Genesis the appearance of light also precedes the appearance of the sun.

A light-burst shines bright in space.

URANUS
Father Heaven

Uranus was the god of heaven. He was the brother of the sea god Pontus. And the earth goddess Gaia chose him for her husband.

Uranus spread himself over Gaia, enveloping her in that comforting way that the sky has on warm spring and summer nights. He dazzled her with stars, fulfilling the dreams that Eros had given her. He swirled through her trees, setting leaves atremble. He wafted across her meadows, freeing milkweed seeds to float everywhere, everywhere. He was tender. That's what she loved the most. That's what made earth and sky harmonious.

They inspired each other, and then Pontus, as well. The three were partners. Soon the lands ran with all manner of wild beasts, the skies hovered with hummingbirds and swooped with falcons, the seas teemed with gleaming fish. Under the beneficent smiles of Gaia and Uranus and Pontus, life in the universe pulsed and whispered and sang.

In those songs, Gaia bore Uranus children, so many children. A flood of sons and daughters—12 in all.

Uranus was overwhelmed. These children were strong and large. And he feared they'd take over the far reaches of the universe. One wanted to play in the deepest swirls of the water. One wanted to shine from on high even brighter than Uranus himself. One wanted to play in the darkest corners of the Underworld.

Distant Planet

The planet Uranus moves slowly and is dim. It consists of icy water, ammonia, and methane gas, surrounded by clouds of mostly hydrogen with a thin outer layer of methane. The outer layer makes Uranus appear blue-green. Winds race across its liquid surface at dizzying speeds. This cold planet is tilted so that its axis of rotation nearly faces the sun. When we look at it through a telescope, its many moons resemble circles around the bull's-eye of a target.

An artist's depiction of the planet Uranus

On top of that, they were unruly. One asked questions incessantly. One acted all high-and-mighty and righteous. One behaved as though she were more motherly than even her bounteous mother Gaia—what presumption! These children were driving Uranus half crazy.

They were too strong. They were too many.

He called them the Titans, which meant "stretchers," because they wanted to stretch themselves in every direction. They wanted power. That was it! That was exactly it. And if they should decide to conspire against him . . .

Uranus shuddered in fear. They were his own children, but his heart turned cold at the very thought of them.

And so he trapped them inside their mother, deep within the recesses of the Earth.

Yet Gaia loved Uranus. She bore him more children, but Uranus' fear poisoned them. They were three sons—strong, yes strapping in fact. But each had only one eye, set in the very middle of his forehead. Uranus called them the Cyclopes, which meant "wheel eyes," and the very sight of them made his mouth go sour. Still Gaia loved Uranus. She bore him more children. By this point Uranus' fear had turned to hatred. The children of such a father couldn't help but be misshapen in hideous ways. They were three more sons, of exceptional power, but each had fifty heads and one hundred arms shooting from his shoulders. Uranus turned his head away, his stomach roiling.

And so Uranus kept them all—all his progeny with Gaia—

Uranus' fear of his Titan children poisoned him so much that his later children were all monstrous, from having only one eye to having a hundred arms and fifty heads.

imprisoned within the crevasses and caverns of the Earth.

Gaia moaned in pain. Her children were thwarted when they should have been thriving. What had happened to tenderness? Where had mercy gone? Her husband had become monstrous.

And so Gaia swallowed her sobs and picked up a great curved blade—the sharpest sickle. She spoke to the children within her. "Your father is evil. Listen to me. Do as I say. Then you can lead free lives."

The children, large as they were, strong as they were, many as they were, huddled together, uncertain. How could their mother say such things? Uranus was their father.

But the youngest Titan, Cronus, didn't huddle. "Mother, I will do the deed." He took the sickle.

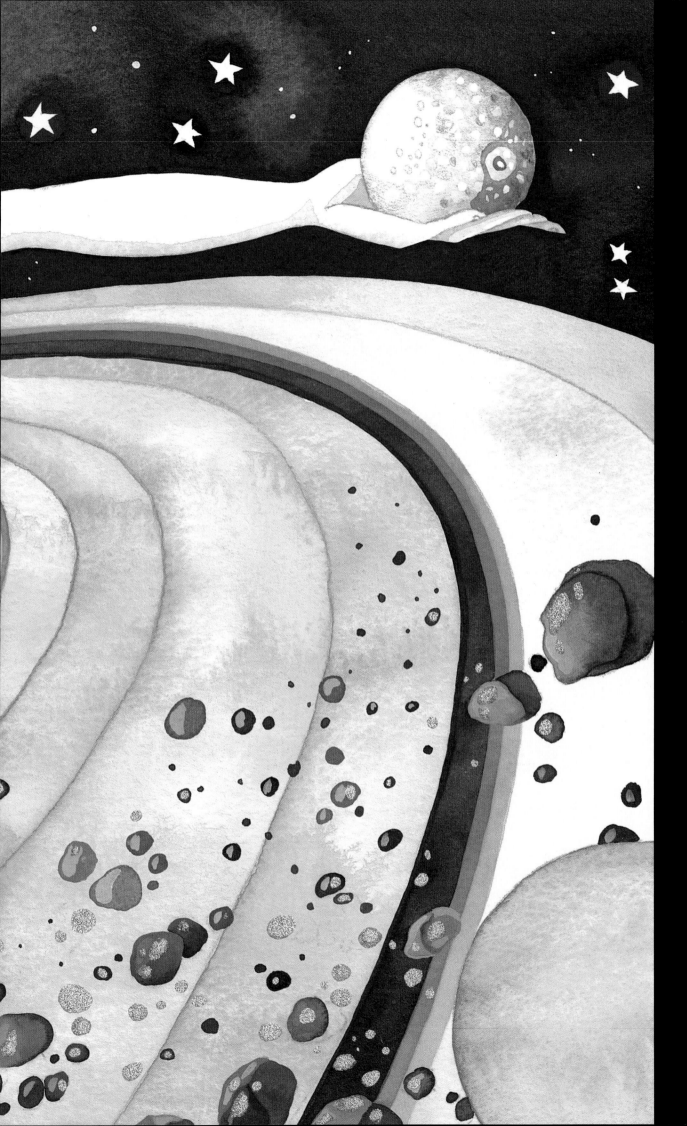

CRONUS
Titan King

Cronus, the Titan son of Gaia, Mother Earth, and Uranus, Father Heaven, lived deep in the Earth, where his father had locked him and his brothers and sisters. While the others quaked in fear at their father and hid in the shadows of their mother, Cronus just watched and listened.

Gaia suffered. The cruelty of this father toward his children was unbearable. She tore her hair, she gnashed her teeth. And in the end, she offered her children an adamantine sickle—lustrous and unbreakable—to confront their father with. Horrified, the children retreated. All but Cronus. Where his courage came from, he didn't know, but he never hesitated. He waited until nightfall, when his father was asleep. Then silently, stealthily, he struck. Wicked Uranus—his fear became a self-fulfilling prophecy. Cruelty is the snake that bites its own tail.

The blow was powerful. Not lethal—no, the old man lived on. But withering—he became a shadow of himself, his strength a memory. An immortal god humiliated for all time.

The blood of Uranus splattered across Gaia. Gaia spun and spun. Yes, she had wanted freedom for her children, yes and yes. But, oh, the cost was so dear. She could do nothing but spin through the whole year. And as she spun the blood drops seeped deep within her. From them sprang three more groups of children.

The furious Erinyes immediately took to the air and flew above Gaia, screaming for vengeance. They were their father's daughters. They wept blood as their serpent hair snapped at the winds.

The giants lumbered forth heavily armed, with breastplates and spears at the ready. They looked around, dazed by their sudden existence, knowing nothing about who was at fault—mother or father, who could know? But one thing was for sure: They had to find a way to wage battle.

The numerous nymphs didn't hesitate; they were their mother's daughters. They ran over the boundless earth, hiding in streams and woodland glades and cool grottoes. They laughed and played, confident already that they would bring delight to a world that so clearly pined for them.

Parts of Uranus splattered across the seas, as well, and thus sprang up the very last child that he would ever father, riding on the sea foam: Aphrodite, who even as a child caused those who viewed her to fall to their knees in wonderment at her beauty.

The sun rising over the horizon

THE RULE of the Titans

Gaia and Uranus had 12 Titan children. Cronus was leader, with Rhea as wife. Oceanus encircled the world in water, while Tethys was mother to land rivers. Hyperion was lord of light, with Theia shining beside him. The other Titans were important mostly because their descendants were remarkable. Titans ruled in the Golden Age but were overthrown by younger gods—the Olympians. One Titan, though—Themis—had lasting importance throughout Greek mythology. She was goddess of right and wrong, embodiment of justice.

Not every little thing was right with the universe, but all was far better than it had been for Cronus and his brothers and sisters; they were free. Cronus crowed at his victory. Both his mother and father looked at him with fear. Each parent, separate and hushed, prophesied to him that he would be stripped of his power by his own son.

The prophecy ate at him, for no one knew better than Cronus the destruction that a child could wreak. He grew sleepless, wild-eyed. Cronus, who had felt no fear as a child, now felt nothing but fear. He distrusted at random, and for no reason at all locked his brothers, the Cyclopes and the hundred-handed ones, in the deepest part of the Underworld, dark Tartarus. He could tolerate the company only of his fellow Titans.

Then his Titan sister Rhea caught his eye. She was too lovely to resist. So he took her as his wife. But each time she gave birth— producing glorious children, the daughters Hestia and Demeter and Hera, the sons Hades and Poseidon—he panicked and swallowed them. Cannibal? No. No no. He told himself this was simply self-protection.

> Cronus' fear of his children transformed his body into their prison— swallow, swallow, five times. But the sixth time he swallowed the swaddled stone and began his own demise.

Rhea, like Gaia before her, felt herself drowning in grief. And, like Gaia before her, she finally reached the dreadful conclusion, the only conclusion: She must stop the brutality.

When she recognized the first stirrings of a new baby within her, she asked her parents, Gaia and Uranus, for help. They shepherded her off to the island of Crete, where she gave birth in secrecy to her son Zeus.

Then she left her newborn son for her mother to raise, swaddled a stone, and hurried home to Cronus, who quickly seized the false babe and swallowed it. Wretched Cronus, completely duped, completely ignorant that his son Zeus lived, completely doomed.

ZEUS
King of the Gods

Young Zeus clambered up the rocks behind a billy goat. He walked the mountain ridge and stopped on the highest peak of Crete to look out over the salt-white sea that stretched to Africa. He turned and there was Gaia, his grandmother, who had raised him.

"You're strong enough," she said. "It's your turn."

Zeus' heartbeat raced. It filled his head. It filled his whole self. He needed no further information or encouragement. His father, Cronus, had swallowed his brothers and sisters at their births. Zeus had escaped only because his mother, Rhea, had fooled the fear-crazed man into swallowing a stone instead. The boy had grown strong, fearsome, clever. He now went quickly to meet his father for the first time. He was primed for this. Armed. This was the moment of defeat or victory, yet his nerves were steady. He felt strangely elated.

While Zeus journeyed, Gaia reached out to Cronus and crooned in rocking tones that penetrated in that deep way only a mother's voice can. The suggestion was too powerful; Cronus doubled over. The stone and children within spewed forth from his mouth, landing at the feet of the newly arrived Zeus.

The five older children of Cronus—Hestia, Poseidon, Hades, Demeter, and Hera—aligned themselves with Zeus against their father. What else could they do? Zeus meant freedom, a delicious new idea.

WARS of Ancient Greece

Mythological wars might reflect stories about real prehistoric wars. The war between the Titans and Olympians lasted ten years, according to the ancient Greek poet Hesiod. Another great war, between Greece and Troy, also lasted ten years, according to the poet Homer. (Poets were often the historians of their age.) We have no information about actual wars from before or during the lives of these poets.

An ancient Greek soldier

But Cronus had brothers and sisters, too. He called the Titans to his side.

War began. And continued, as wars will do. For ten years the battle scorched the earth, smoked the skies, sullied the waters. Bitter as bile, it wore away at everyone's spirits. Until Gaia, the earth mother who had started all life, told Zeus he would win if he liberated her other children—his misshapen uncles and his one-eyed uncles—that Cronus had cast into Tartarus, the Underworld.

Zeus never wasted a moment on second thoughts. He freed the three brothers with fifty heads and one hundred hands each. He freed the three Cyclopes. In surprised gratitude, the Cyclopes gave Zeus the spitting lightning bolt and deafening thunder with which to split the skies and flame the earth. They gave his brothers gifts, too. On Poseidon they bestowed a sharp, gleaming trident with which to smite the seabeds and raise massive waves. To Hades they gave a helmet of invisibility with which to disappear.

These hundred-handed and one-eyed brothers fought beside their nieces and nephews, all against the Titans. And the nephews let loose with their newly gained ferocity. No longer was the battle simply hurling rocks and spears, and crushing the enemy with axes. Oh, no. Zeus hurled bolts, burned the forests, and left them smoldering. He cast flames so hot the seas boiled and parts of the Earth melted. Poseidon shook the Earth so rivers crashed through their sidewalls. Hades raced unseen among all, stabbing, smashing, maiming.

As Zeus saw it, the war amounted to old against young, and the young gods won, as they had to. That is the nature of things. By the end of the war, both sets of gods fought from mountaintops—the Titans from Mount Othrys, the young gods from Mount Olympus. So after the war the young gods were known as the Olympians.

Zeus had the Titans sealed in Tartarus with the hundred-handed ones as guards. Gaia was flummoxed. What was the point of locking away the Titans? Why did Zeus have to be as vengeful as his father? And so she gave birth to her last child, the monster Typhon. From his shoulders sprang a

Gaia gave birth to the monster Typhon, hoping he could stand up to his bully brother Zeus. But the weapon of the thunderbolt allowed Zeus to conquer Typhon's hundred heads.

hundred serpentine heads with flickering black tongues uttering every noise imaginable—human, bestial, thunderous. Typhon's eyes flashed fire. Everyone fell back in terror. Except Zeus. He had lightning, a force unsurpassed. He burned off Typhon's heads and banished him to become wild winds that cursed sailors on the high seas. Zeus was the undisputed king.

The Olympian brothers divided up rulership of the universe. Poseidon took the seas; Hades, the Underworld; Zeus, everything else. The division wasn't equal, and the Olympian sisters were left out entirely. But that was typical of Zeus. He was brought up to believe he was entitled. Nothing ever changed his mind.

HESTIA Goddess of the Hearth

HESTIA
Goddess of the Hearth

Hestia's first memory was of blackness. And stifling heat. Then something tumbled in beside her, all wiggly. And another wiggly something. And two more. And, finally, a giant lump. She was crowded, poked and prodded, cramped. And so breathlessly, unrelentingly hot. She didn't know she was trapped in her father Cronus' belly. She didn't know the wiggly somethings around her were her sisters Demeter and then Hera, and her brothers Hades and then Poseidon. She didn't know the lump was a stone her father had been duped into swallowing in place of his sixth child. She knew only great discomfort and an undefined lack that gnawed at her spirit. Something was supposed to be happening. Someone was supposed to be there. Somehow everything was wrong, everything hurt. A vague fear lodged in her heart.

Then came a constriction so tight and forceful, Hestia screamed, there in the place with no air. Silent and pained, she screamed and screamed until her throat was raw, and she was pushed up and up and out. She lay, disgorged on the ground, with brothers and sisters and that one stone, blinking at the rude light of day, shrinking from the edginess of the noises carried through the air, wet and shivering and shocked to be separate from the four other wiggly bodies and the lump of a stone.

GENTLE Goddess

Hestia is a mysterious figure; she appears only as the goddess prayed to about family matters. The ancient Greeks seemed to hold family concerns private, separate from the usual squabbles of their stories. The earliest records of family law in Greece are the codes of Gortyn in Crete in 450 B.C., which concern finances; they don't tell how an ordinary family should behave at home. Probably the father ruled, given how royal households in Greek mythology behaved. But that's just a guess.

A temple dedicated to Hestia, illustrated on an ancient coin

Her brother Zeus had freed them, strange thing that he was, all tanned and muscular and accustomed to everything Hestia found so foreign. He freed them, only to tell them they must fight at his side against their father Cronus and his sister and brother Titans. Rocks, spears, axes. Shouts, cries, howls. Freed into a war? This was freedom? Was the world insane?

Hestia cringed. She picked up rocks in both hands and feigned interest whenever others watched her, but, fortunately, they rarely did. She climbed trees and peeked through their thick foliage, hoping for a glimpse of her mother Rhea, of the arms that had never cradled her, the hands that had never caressed her. She built a mound of stones with a pit in the middle and sat there hidden, wondering when the sweat and blood and tears would ever stop, and, if they did, who she would then be. For up to this point, she had been no one, really.

And then it ended. But not because the animosity had run its course. No. It ended because her brother Zeus got the

Ancient Greek
families took
consolation from
knowing Hestia
watched over
their daily home
life in the gentlest
of ways. And Hestia
found peace in
giving that
consolation.

help of strange men with fifty heads and a hundred arms, and because other strange men with a single eye in the middle of their foreheads gave Zeus the lightning bolt—the great cheat. That's how the war ended—with one side getting a weapon the other had no equal of. Cheat cheat cheat.

Hestia's brothers were impressed with Zeus' power. Poseidon was only too happy to rule the seas, Hades was only too happy to rule the Underworld, and both were only too happy to leave the rest to Zeus.

Hestia's sisters were impressed with Zeus' tanned skin and muscled legs and arms and chest and back. Each looked at him with flirty eyes.

Only Hestia saw Zeus as a frightful maniac. She kept her distance from him and all other males, like a shy spider.

She looked everywhere, and she saw the families the Titans had formed over the years, and she saw the families their children were forming and the families their grandchildren were forming, and she saw a kind of love that made her ache. They sat around the hearth eating and talking and teasing with one another. They hugged and laughed. That love—that was what Hestia wanted to foster in the world. And so Hestia became the goddess of hearth and home, and in her quiet, still way she finally banished the fear from her heart and found a gentle, soothing peace.

POSEIDON
God of the Seas

Poseidon, along with his brother Hades, and his sisters Hestia and Demeter and Hera, was swallowed at birth by his father Cronus. Then a sixth child, Zeus, who was never swallowed, and thus had never known humiliation, freed them. Poseidon sized things up: Zeus was a force to be reckoned with—that was the guy to follow.

For ten long years, the six brothers and sisters fought their father and aunts and uncles—the mighty Titans. It was a nasty war, but what war isn't? Poseidon gritted his teeth and did his part. He was no coward, after all. He donned armor and went dutifully into battle. He never lagged.

But now and then there was a lull in the battle, perhaps because Zeus got distracted or because the Titans, despite their huge size, needed a rest. Who knew? No one ever explained things to Poseidon. Whatever the case, Poseidon was grateful, and in those moments he took refuge in visiting Pontus, the ancient god of all the waters, the partner to his grandmother Gaia, Mother Earth, and his grandfather Uranus, Father Heaven. He swam in Pontus' waters, and, despite how badly his life had gone so far, despite all the time locked up in his father's belly, despite all the long years of savage war, he was happy. He found joy in the buoyancy of diving whales, he found beauteous rhythm in the undulating wake of eels, he found humor in the scuttling of crabs.

Best of all, Poseidon found a friend in the oldest son of Pontus and Gaia. His name was Nereus, and he loved the watery depths as much as Poseidon did. Together they plunged to the corals and sponges that lived on the seabed. They rode on the backs of turtles. They flapped their arms like the rays they followed, then let them hang with their legs moving at the whim of the currents like the tentacles of the nearly transparent jellyfish.

But then it was back to war, until the glorious moment when the hundred-handed sons of Gaia joined the battle on Zeus' side, and then the Cyclopes gave Zeus the thunderbolt and Hades the helmet that made him invisible and Poseidon the trident. It worked, that trident. It worked splendidly. Poseidon struck it on the ground and the earth shook, boulders tumbled to the sea, rivers overflowed their banks. Ha! The Olympian gods won.

And Zeus appointed Poseidon ruler of the seas. Poseidon knew his brother felt the seas were an inferior realm to rule. Ha again! Nothing could have pleased Poseidon more.

WATER Gods

The sea god Triton at the Trevi Fountain in Rome

Many gods ruled the waters beside Pontus, Nereus, and Poseidon. Poseidon's son Triton trumpeted the noises of moving water. His son Proteus changed shape at will—as seas seemed to do to the ancient Greeks. The Titan Oceanus was a continuous water loop: the connected system of the Earth's five oceans. Then there were saltwater nymphs (Nereids), freshwater nymphs (Naiads), and three mortals who became sea divinities. The variety of gods may reflect ancient Greek knowledge of the complexities of the water systems.

With his black mane flying out behind him, he swam the seas in search of those who might need his help. It was a welcome antidote to that tedious war. And when he wasn't patrolling, he let himself be absorbed in the watery mysteries.

That's when he discovered the finest mystery ever. She was the granddaughter of Pontus and Gaia, and the daughter of the lordly sea god Phorcys and the lovely cheeked sea goddess Ceto. That heritage made her the perfect wife in Poseidon's eyes. She was one of three sisters, called the Gorgons. The other two sisters were immortal, like the gods. But Medusa, as she was called, was mortal.

Poseidon found her mortality that much more alluring. She was vulnerable. How amazing to know someone vulnerable. He put his arms out and let the serpents of her hair swarm around them. Good! Those serpents could bite and poison—good protection. He gingerly touched the wings that jutted from her shoulder blades. Good good! Those wings could carry her far from an attacker. He stroked her scales. Ah, very good indeed! They were harder than armor. And most assuring of all, she had a special power: Anything mortal that looked directly at her face would turn instantly to stone. That should do it.

And so Poseidon felt almost safe in loving Medusa. They reveled together in his sea kingdom. At least for a while.

Humans who viewed Medusa's ugly face turned to stone. Yet Poseidon found her wonderful and fell passionately in love, caressed by her serpent hair in the deep ocean waters.

ATHENA
Goddess of Wisdom

During the period when Cronus ruled the world, the Titans lived large, some on the land and some in the seas. The deepest oceans were the haunt of Oceanus, a Titan brimming with the need to spread his waters everywhere. His sister Tethys swam beside him, lithe, graceful, and white-haired. Not gray—she was not aged. Not silver—she was not a source of light. True white. Pure as mother's milk. It was that white hair that had captured Oceanus. He took Tethys as his wife.

Together they created so many sons, all strong rivers, from the great Nile of Egypt, to the famous Skamander of Troy, to the many that emptied into the friendly Black Sea. They swirled in eddies, they rippled with gusto, they rushed over cliffs and fell in loud, energetic sheets to the rocks below.

Then Oceanus and Tethys created so many daughters, all water nymphs, some inhabiting pools in foothills, some splashing in springs, some slipping through swamps. Each nymph was unique: one rosy, one nimble, one soft-eyed, one knowing—all charming.

When Zeus, the youngest son of Cronus, deposed his father and took his place on the throne as king of the universe, his eye fell on one of these nymphs, and he was indeed charmed. Metis, known as the wise one, seemed to flow like water to Zeus, cool and soothing. Watching her was

BIRTHPLACE of Democracy

Athena gave the olive tree to a special city, thereafter named Athens. Around 500 B.C., Athens decided citizens should vote. Democracy was born! But women were not included. Men had many powers unique to them. The only power unique to women was childbearing. In the Athena myth, Athena is born from Zeus' forehead. Certainly the Greeks knew men don't give birth. But maybe they wished men did, for Uranus, Cronus, and Zeus, each in his own way, tried to take this power from womanhood.

Olive trees in front of ancient ruins in Athens, Greece

like swimming in a clear, bubbling spring. He was smitten. And since he was king and felt he deserved anything he wanted, he simply took her as his wife. Metis soon had a child growing within her.

That's when Zeus' grandmother Gaia and grandfather Uranus gave him the ugly warning that, by now, he almost expected: Metis would bear him a daughter and then a son, and the son would be invincible. That splendid son, that wretched and hateful son, he would overcome his father. The curse felt never-ending: Uranus was overcome by his son Cronus, Cronus was overcome by his son Zeus, and now Zeus would be overcome by the son that Metis was fated to bear him.

Zeus would have none of it. His grandfather Uranus had tried to prevent his overthrow by imprisoning his children

A baby within a mother within a father—that's who Athena was—doubly trapped. But she sprang forth against the odds; as goddess of wisdom, she was no one's prisoner.

inside their mother Gaia. A failed attempt. His father Cronus had tried to prevent his overthrow by imprisoning his children inside himself. Another failed attempt. Zeus was smarter than either of them. He opened his mouth wide and drank Metis—simply drank her, like a glass of the best sparkling water in the world. So long as she was trapped inside him, he could never make a son with her, so the prophecy was null and void.

Zeus went on to take other wives, a long series of them. And all the while within him Metis sloshed around the growing babe, rocking her lovingly. And the baby experienced the world from inside her mother inside her father. She sensed everything that either of them sensed. She grew wiser than both.

Time passed and Zeus felt queasy, as though his stomach would burst. Then the pressure moved to behind his eyes and nearly blinded him. His temples throbbed. His hair stood on end. And from his forehead sprang the goddess Athena, whole and solid and heavily armed.

The gray-eyed girl looked around, completely alert and completely wise. She took her place among the Olympian gods and watched, with those gray gray eyes, ever ready for the chance to advise the belligerent, to strategize with warriors, to lead soldiers into battle.

HADES
God of the Underworld

One image had engraved itself in the mind of young, trapped Hades: the gaping hole of his father's mouth, the yellow of his teeth, the stench of his breath as the huge man swallowed him. From within his father's belly he punched now and then at the old man's liver. Remember us, he beat out with his fists, remember your evil act.

When the young gods and goddesses finally spilled out amid the loud groans of their retching father, Hades scrambled to his feet and shook his fists at the rudeness of bright daylight. He'd grown accustomed to the dark, plus he was spitting mad.

So roaring into war beside his siblings felt natural—like butter on a burn—it felt fat and rich and right. He fought like the maddened against his father and the rest of the Titans. And when the Cyclopes joined the battle and presented gifts, Hades didn't hesitate. He jammed the magic helmet on his head. He flew high, then bombed down like a falcon, straight for the back of Cronus' neck. He slashed and slashed, flaying the old man's flesh, always unseen, like in the old days inside the hateful one, but this time effectual. It was Hades who truly overcame the most blame-ridden father of the universe. Hades brought Cronus to his knees; Hades brought Cronus to justice. Wickedness deserves to crawl through the slime.

When Zeus was about to hand out realms, Hades again didn't wait. He declared the Underworld his. It was the land of darkness, and in all those years of war, Hades had never learned to like daylight. And it was the land of justice. It was where the ruling god sent those gods who fell out of favor with him, the wicked gods. Hades would deal with the wicked. And show no mercy.

He sat upon an anvil of bronze and fell from the surface of the Earth for nine days and nine nights, until he landed in the Underworld. He could have simply willed himself there. But it pleased him to experience the enormous distance. No one would bother him down here; he was absolute ruler.

The Underworld was huge. Had Hades wanted, he could have fallen another year before landing at the very bottom. But he didn't. The knowledge of its vastness was enough. He visited Night, one of the earliest powers, draped over his walls, so nicely obscuring. He crossed over Styx, the cold

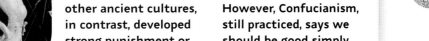

VISIONS of an Afterlife

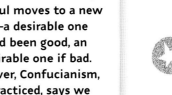

After death, mortals wandered the misty gloom of Hades' House. Only a few terrible sinners were tormented, and even fewer heroes were rewarded. Many other ancient cultures, in contrast, developed strong punishment or reward visions of the afterlife to encourage good behavior in this life. Others proposed reincarnation: After death, the soul moves to a new body—a desirable one if you'd been good, an undesirable one if bad. However, Confucianism, still practiced, says we should be good simply because that's the right thing to do.

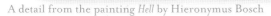

A detail from the painting *Hell* by Hieronymus Bosch

river of hate, the oldest daughter of the Titan Oceanus, who had been given a glorious palace in Tartarus for siding with Zeus in the war against the Titans. He passed by Atlas, the dimwitted son of Iapetus, half brother to the Titans. Atlas had sided with the Titans in the long war, so Zeus doomed him for eternity to bear on the nape of his neck and the girdle of his shoulders the entire weight of the heavens. He passed by the Hesperides, daughters of Night, guarding a tree of golden apples.

The River Styx flows mean and cold, past the aching shoulders of Atlas, while the beautiful Hesperides watch for would-be thieves and the ferryman Charon waits for the newly dead.

This was a fitting realm for him, indeed, especially since now and forever he could keep an eye on that scum-of-a-father Cronus and make sure he never knew freedom again.

With a satisfied sigh, Hades entered his stone palace and looked out on the ghostly and frigid fields, where colorless asphodels bent to a chilling wind. It felt strange to be so alone. He'd have to fix that. Soon.

DEMETER
Goddess of the Harvest

Zeus, the king of the Olympian gods, married a nymph goddess, Metis, and wound up swallowing her to avoid her ever having a son who might overpower him. From their union came Athena, an Olympian goddess. Then Zeus married a Titan, Themis, and had a number of children who cared about justice and peace and government. Then he married another nymph, Eurynome, a sister to his first wife, and she bore him three daughters with cheeks as round and fresh as apples, called the Graces.

And then Zeus took a fourth wife. Ah, yes, his fourth wife. She was his sister, the goddess Demeter. None of Zeus' wives were frivolous, yet none were anywhere near as solid as Demeter. Her hair was the rich gold of ripening wheat. Her fragrant shoulder was a welcoming cushion for a baby's head. All she needed to do was smile and fruit trees blossomed and bore so many sweetnesses that they bent nearly to the earth with their abundance. All she needed to do was glance lovingly and greens shot up from the loamy soil and spread thick, dark, nourishing leaves. She was the goddess of the bountiful harvest, and the whole world counted on her generosity. She made Zeus feel cared for, safe—like his grandmother Gaia had made him feel. Perhaps Gaia sensed this; perhaps she felt a small tingle of jealousy.

Demeter bore to Zeus a single daughter, Persephone. The girl had thin arms, pearl white. She gave off the scent

THE MARCH of Seasons

The Earth is tilted on its axis. The part oriented toward the sun is hot; the part oriented away is cold. As the Earth circles the sun, the part oriented toward the sun changes. That is why we have seasons. The Equator, being midway, has a consistent orientation, so climate there is nearly uniform. The ancient Greeks looked at seasons and used myths to explain their mystery. In many ancient cultures, myth originated to account for other baffling natural phenomena.

Earth and the rising sun

of night jasmine. Light played on her face, making her appear as varied and rich with colors as a meadow of flowers. Her ankles were slight, adding grace to agility. Demeter doted on her. How could she not?

Persephone played often with the nymph daughters of Oceanus, for they were all of like mind, laughing, lithesome lovelies. One day they gamboled through soft grasses decorated with narcissi, crocuses, violets, irises, hyacinths. And the Olympian god Hades, from the Underworld below, noticed Persephone's ankles, those trim little things. Those quick little things. There was nothing in Tartarus quite like them. Delicate delicate ankles, spiderwebs glistening with dew in a forest dawn.

Hades was enamored of her. But she was his brother Zeus' daughter. So he spoke of his love to Zeus, the king who knew next to nothing about a father's duty. How could he, being the son of Cronus, the great swallower? Zeus left the raising of his many children to his many wives. So Zeus turned to Gaia, Mother Earth, for help. Gaia should have known better than to be lured in. But maybe that tingle came to her again. Maybe her eyes smarted just a little at the very name of Demeter. Gaia put forth a most radiant flower from the center of her being, a single root with a hundred blossoms whose perfume wafted over the far seas.

Persephone didn't have a chance. She reached for the treasure and—oh!— the earth opened and Hades grabbed her. Snatched. Gone.

Demeter sped like a wild bird over land and sea, searching. She ate nothing, drank nothing, slept not at all. Her cheeks grew hollow, her body gaunt. Greens turned brown. Fruits withered to dust. Hunger twisted the innards of every living creature. And all this time Zeus simply watched.

But Hecate, the great-granddaughter of two Titans, had pity and told Demeter what had happened. Demeter shrank in upon herself, biting her own fists in rage and frustration. Not until life on Earth was threatened with imminent famine did Zeus finally send his winged son Hermes to fetch the girl.

And so Persephone was returned to Demeter. But Hades had put in her mouth a single pomegranate seed and the winsome girl had swallowed it. Alas. Because she had tasted anything, even this tiny morsel, on her brief and miserable stint in the Underworld, she was obliged to spend a third of every year

there as Hades' wife. The other two-thirds of the year, she spent with her mother Demeter.

Hence the Earth sprouts and flowers and fruits through spring and summer and autumn, when Demeter and Persephone hold hands in the fields. But the world turns bare and unyielding through winter, when Persephone returns to Hades and bereft Demeter mourns.

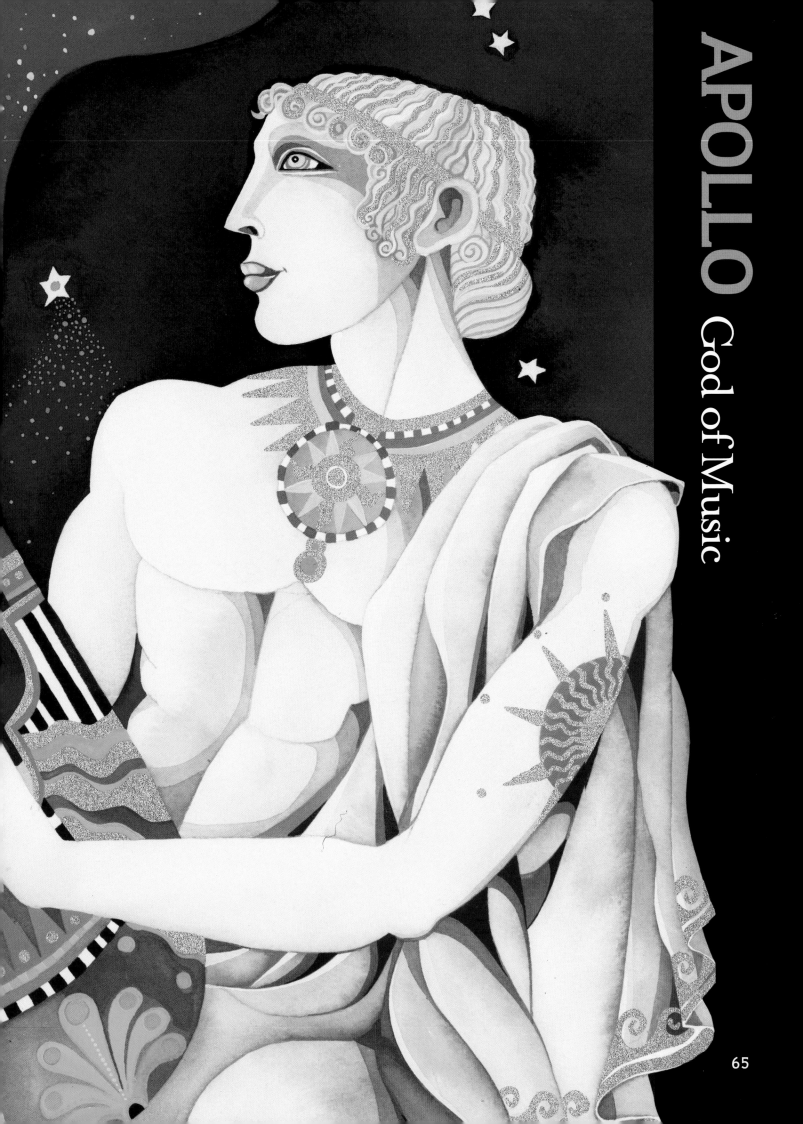

APOLLO
God of Music

Leto, the daughter of Titans, walked in black robes. Not because she didn't like colors. No, she adored colors. Leto's favorite thing was walking after a downpour under a sky made marvelous by the trick of Iris and Helios. Iris was the granddaughter of Pontus and a Titan, and Helios, the sun itself, was the child of Titans. They made the heavens arch with rainbows. The desperate felt hopeful, the timid felt emboldened, the bold grew ready to charge. But Leto didn't want to raise hopes herself, nor embolden others, nor be the target of a charge. Colors uplifted the spirit, but also agitated it. Black was kinder; black settled the spirit.

So it wasn't her fault when Zeus' eye fell on her. Everyone knew Zeus' eye obeyed no limits. He was a brash, entitled, bossy fellow. Yet somehow Leto felt sympathy for him. It couldn't be easy ruling the universe. Her fingertips fluttered on his cheeks and she cried inside for him. Besides, he was beautiful—so she accepted him as her husband.

When she found herself with child, she looked for a suitable birthing place. She expected welcome everywhere; this was Zeus' child inside her. Instead, she was closed out. Rumor had it that the child would grow to be feared as much as Zeus. What? Gentle Leto would bear a god who made others tremble? How could it be? Certainly, some land somewhere would know this was a good child. She walked the earth, round and round, until her feet felt like stumps.

And then the pains came. They started in her belly, but they moved swiftly to her back. Excruciating. The goddess Hera, Zeus' sister, came and put her arms around Leto and took her up to Mount Olympus. Hera whispered comfortingly. She pushed Leto's lovely tresses away from her face and put cooling compresses on her cheeks and forehead. Leto understood Hera's acts for what they were: the product of envy. Hera had become Zeus' next wife shortly after he'd been with Leto. But Hera was not yet with child. It didn't matter why Hera was helping her, though. Leto clung to her in raw need.

For nine days and nights Leto's body struggled with the pains of labor. Then it dawned on her: Water! She needed to float in water. She rolled down the mountain to the sea, and the waves washed her to the little island of Ortygia, where a daughter, Artemis, slipped from her as easy as a stream

THE DANCING Muses

Apollo is god of many things, including music, poetry, and other arts. He often walked with the Muses: nine graceful daughters of Zeus and the Titan Mnemosyne. Calliope inspired poets to write epic poems; Erato, love poems; Euterpe, nature poems. Thalia gave humor to those who wanted to cause laughter; Melpomene gave insight to those who wanted to cause tears. Urania helped people understand stars and planets; Clio helped them understand the past. Terpsichore led her sisters in dance, and Polyhymnia led the songs.

Dancing muses from a painting by Baldassare Peruzzi

Leto gave birth to the fast-growing Artemis on one island, then to her twin, Apollo, on another island. The second island was rocky and barren, but became a lush garden the moment the young god was born.

running downhill. What relief! They set out traveling over sea back to Olympus, so Leto could present Artemis to her father. Yet almost instantly the pains returned. Leto barely made it to the rugged Isle of Delos in time. She dragged herself up the Cynthian Hill, her daughter tied to her chest, and, still kneeling, cast her arms around a lone palm tree, whereupon a second child came forth, leaping into the light.

Apollo! His very cry was music. He was strong and beautiful. Faultless.

"Faultless," came the chorus that echoed Leto's thought. For all the goddesses had gathered, from the shyest nymph to grand Gaia. Zeus had had many children by many wives, but this was the first son, a true cause for celebration. They washed the boy, and swathed him in white, and fastened a golden band around him.

The rocky Isle of Delos burst into bloom with flowers of every color, challenging the rainbow.

Nearly overnight Apollo grew into everything his father hoped. He declared himself unswervingly loyal to Zeus and carried with him a bow and arrows to protect the will of his father. No one dared cross this archer, who never missed a mark. Yet there was something of his mother in him still. In peaceful moments, he played the lyre his younger half brother Hermes gave him. And he often called to his side the Muses, nine daughters of Zeus and the Titan Mnemosyne, who sang with harp voices that resonated in listeners' hearts and danced with light, agile feet that made the surface of the Earth move in rhythm. Apollo saw them as his personal ornaments. And he often rode with the sun god Helios, source of colors, in his chariot across the wide sky. Apollo fancied himself as bright as the sun, and since he'd been born on the seventh day of the week, thereafter that day became known as Sunday.

Leto doted on Apollo. When he was tired, she'd unstring his bow, close his quiver, and hang all on a golden peg in Zeus' palace. She'd bid him sit and patted his shoulder while Zeus gave him nectar in a golden cup. It's no surprise that Apollo became the haughtiest of gods.

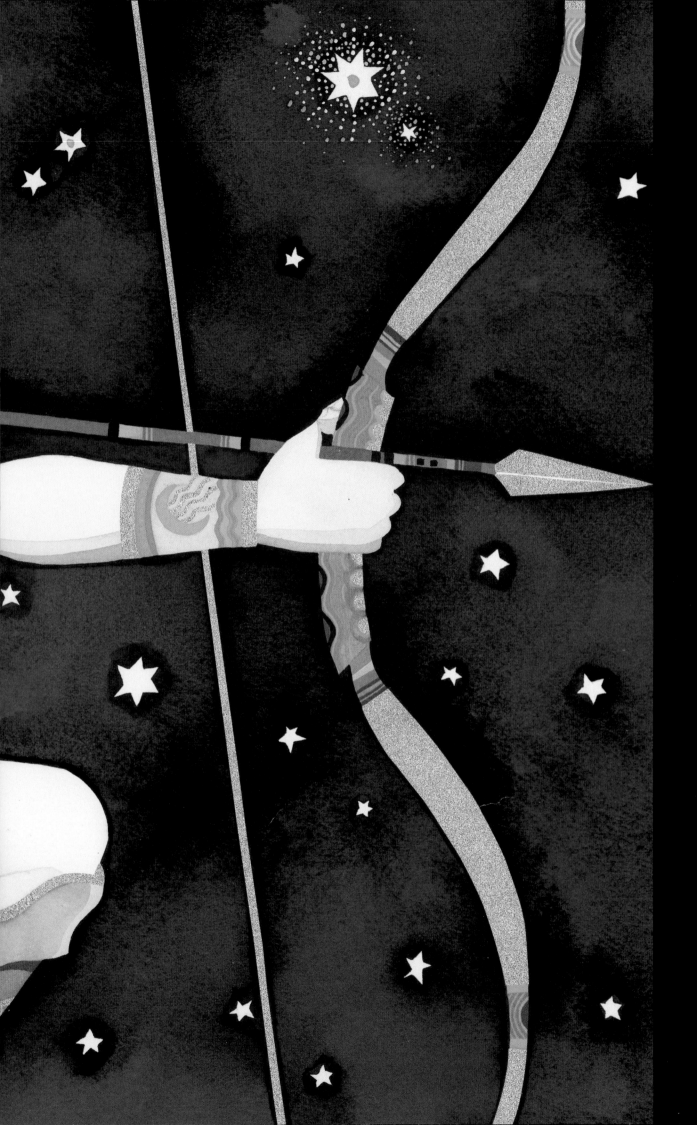

ARTEMIS Goddess of the Hunt

ARTEMIS
Goddess of the Hunt

All that fuss about Apollo's birth didn't faze Artemis. She was the older twin, anyway. Besides, love was not a fixed pie, to be divided up and then gone. Her parents Leto and Zeus both adored her. As for the rest of the gods, Artemis couldn't really have cared less who they praised or didn't. She felt no need for flattery.

While Apollo was almost instantly an adult, Artemis enjoyed her childhood. As a bud of a girl, she sat on Zeus' lap and asked for a bow and arrows. Not huge, obvious, threatening things like the ones Apollo carried. She wanted slender silver arrows and a small, sweetly curving bow. But she didn't want anyone to get confused and think she herself was sweet. When her father presented her with these gifts, she gave his beard a quick yank rather than a dainty kiss. And when the great smithy god pulled her onto his knee, she plucked out the hairs on his chest, making the poor god

look a bit like a dog with mange. No one could predict what Artemis might do next.

And while her brother went in white, trying to make everyone confuse him with the sun god Helios, Artemis wore stylish high boots and a short tunic of many colors, and men looked at her. They said she was as dreamy as the moon goddess Selene. Though she didn't invite their glances, it felt good to be watched.

Her brother surrounded himself with the nine Muses. Artemis surrounded herself with innumerable sea nymphs and wood nymphs. Plus she had swift hounds, some half white that nearly disappeared they ran so fast, some with hanging ears that fluttered like feathers, and one all speckled brown and pink like a quail egg. Together they hunted rabbit and porcupine and gazelle and lynx and stag. No, this young goddess was never lonely.

Artemis never married, but she was rarely alone. Dogs and sea nymphs and wood nymphs ran with her on the hunt through woods as prey fled from the famed archer.

And, unlike Apollo, she never sought the praise of people. She preferred, in fact, to keep her distance from them, holding hands with her retinue of nymphs in wide circle dances that made the very mountains shiver with pleasure.

It was only when birthing women found their labor pains too great that she entered cities; for there was something about her that eased newborns' way. It was natural, she guessed. Hadn't she herself flowed from her mother like a good wish, after all? She would put on gold armor and travel in her golden chariot pulled by brawny bucks with towering antlers, all bridled with gold, all caught by her with nothing but her bare hands, and spare these women so much grief. Now that was something worth getting praised for.

But not all women recognized they owed their good fortune in childbearing to Artemis. One of the ungrateful was Niobe, daughter of the god Tantalus. She and her husband Amphion, a son of Zeus, had six brave and strong sons and six beautiful and graceful daughters. Niobe crowed with pride. She claimed the people of Thebes should make offerings to her, rather than to Leto, the mother of Apollo and Artemis. It made sense to Niobe: She had twelve children when Leto had only two. She vastly underestimated the danger of making Leto her rival.

Leto went complaining straight to her children, both famed archers. Apollo tracked down Niobe's sons as they

WARRIOR Women

In Greek mythology Amazons were skillful archers who lived without men—like Artemis. But unlike the hunter Artemis, they were warriors on horseback. While many scholars call them fictitious, the Greek historian Herodotus claimed they are based on ancestors to the Sarmatians, living from the fifth to the fourth century B.C., whose women rode into battle beside men. Others see their origin in tribes in southern Ukraine and Russia, or in Crete during Minoan times, all cultures that had women warriors.

An Amazon warrior on horseback

hunted on Mount Cithaeron. He shot arrows into all. Artemis wouldn't let Niobe get off that easily, though. Only the cruelest of acts could make it clear that gods would tolerate no challenges. Artemis wanted the mother to witness each arrow as it hit the mark. She entered Niobe's home and shot arrows into her girls.

Niobe sank to the ground like a stone. But again she was not allowed even this cold end. This bereft mother wasn't a senseless stone; no, no, she felt arrows hit her children over and over. She cried forever, a constant fountain. That sent a message, all right.

Apollo could do what he wanted. But Artemis was a force to be reckoned with in her own right. Women knew it. That was enough for her.

HERA
Goddess of Marriage

Hera was the daughter of Cronus and Rhea, so she had gotten off to a bad start—swallowed by her father and all. But she didn't think much about her early life. Nor did she care much about the interminable war between the Olympians and the Titans that commenced almost immediately after she and her siblings were freed from their papa's belly. No, none of that mattered. Life really started for Hera when she put on her gold sandals and strutted before that brother of hers, Zeus, and, oh glorious moment, he looked at her in that way of his. She felt awakened, energized. He was a handsome devil. But, oh, he turned out to be a troublesome devil.

It would have been a jewel in her crown if she'd been his first wife. But, then, Zeus drank his first wife—that ill-fated nymph, Metis. And they called her wise. Ha! So no, no no no, better not to have been the first.

But then he went on to a Titan wife—with a body larger than his, imagine!—and then another nymph, and then, of all things, her own sister Demeter, and next he took Leto, the daughter of Titans. This devilish god was worse than a billy goat, and he was driving Hera to distraction. Most mortifying of all, that doe-eyed Leto bore him a son! It was Hera who should have borne his first son! Everything was going wrong.

But Hera played it smart. No one should guess her smoldering anger. She wore an innocent maiden's smile and carried herself as though basking in the admiration of the whole world. Everyone fell for it; she must be a beauty if she walked like that. And Zeus fell harder than anyone; he called Hera the most precious blossom he'd ever seen. She pinched her cheeks to darken them, as if with the blush of modesty, and she looked out at him from under long lashes. He needed her. But she wouldn't yield until he made her not just his wife, but his queen. Queen Hera. The only true wife of King Zeus.

Zeus was hers, at last.

Vengeful, envious Hera knew how to play the blushing, comely bride. Selfish Zeus demanded any lovely he wanted. He crowned Hera queen, and they each got their just rewards.

But what did he do? Without missing a beat, he moved from Hera's embrace to the embrace of Maia, the daughter of that stupid Atlas, who bore the heavens on his shoulder girdle, and the granddaughter of Titans. Hera could predict the future: one simpering female after another in Zeus' arms. It was revolting, actually. She vowed then and there to have revenge on every single future rival, into eternity. In fact, she would teach a lesson to anyone who helped Zeus meet other wives. Her punishments would be severe; they'd give pause. So there, Zeus.

And then the very worst thing happened.

Zeus had drunk that first wife Metis and no one had ever given her another thought. But now, so long afterward, Zeus doubled over in pain and the next thing Hera knew, this . . . this thing . . . burst from his forehead. A goddess, in full armor. Zeus had given birth to his daughter Athena all on his own.

Oh, that wasn't really the case. No one could believe that. A male had no such powers. Females were the ones who could have babies. Hera's grandfather had tried to stop her grandmother from giving birth by forcing the children to stay inside their mother. Hera's father had tried to rob her mother of the benefits of giving birth by swallowing her babies as they were born. And now Hera's husband, who was also her brother and thus the inheritor of such malicious behavior, had claimed the ability of giving birth for himself. It was all part of one giant effort to strip women of their most important power. Ridiculous! Athena was the result of Metis giving birth inside Zeus. She was not the product of Zeus alone. No!

Though every other insult was hateful, this one was truly intolerable. In a rage, Hera closed in upon herself, concentrating all her energies on one tiny dot within her. Her grandmother Gaia had done it before her. Need. It was all a question of need. Hera practically melted with need. And, yes! Triumph! Life began within her—and this time it really was all on her own. A woman could do it all on her own. Hera would give birth to the god Hephaestus, her first child and the one that would be totally and completely hers. No matter what Zeus did, he couldn't rob her of that.

HERA'S Revenge

Hera was always furious at Zeus' romances. One was with the priestess Io. Zeus turned Io into a white cow to protect her from Hera. But Hera asked Zeus for the cow as a gift, and she made the giant Argus guard her. Argus had a hundred eyes; some eyes slept while others kept watch. Zeus had Hermes kill Argus and free Io. In grief, Hera set Argus' eyes in the peacock's tail. And she sent a gadfly to torment Io and drive her away from Zeus.

A peacock displaying his tail

HEPHAESTUS God of Metalworking

HEPHAESTUS
God of Metalworking

Hera, the queen of the gods, was angry at Zeus. Again. He was an inconstant and unloving husband, and she'd just about had it. Then he went and produced a daughter from his forehead. The pompous nitwit. So Hera decided to show him. She produced life all on her own, too. Even when it was still tiny and nestled within her, she knew it was a boy. Ha! He'd rival Zeus' son Apollo. Ha ha ha!

And then Hephaestus was born. Oh. Hera's face went slack. Oh, that foot. That tiny, twisted, shriveled foot. Her hand recoiled. She stepped away from the babe. This was too much to bear. Her first child, created solely from her, and now he was a weak, useless thing. This thing shamed her. It disgraced her. With a shriek, she grabbed the child by his pitiful heel and cast him out, far far, into the wide and wild seas, forever lost.

But he didn't fall lost, despite Hera's wishes. The lovely silver-footed Thetis held out her hands and caught the babe. Her father was Nereus, the son of Pontus. Her mother was Doris, the daughter of Oceanus. Thetis was born to the watery world and knew very well how to manage life there. She enclosed Hephaestus in a bubble of her own breath and brought him to a sea cave where he grew strong in her love.

The sea creatures laughed at his funny foot. And when Hephaestus was grown and walked haltingly upon the land with the help of a cane, the land creatures pointed in derision,

Father of Invention

Hera scorned Hephaestus' shriveled foot. Others laughed at him. Ugly attitudes toward differences from the norm were common in ancient cultures. The early Israelites, for example, believed afflictions proved you'd done something wrong. Even today some cultures believe that. But the ancient Greeks recognized a healthy mind regardless. Hephaestus is known as the father of invention. He made the first wheelchair in literature, although the first record of a wheelchair used by a human was on a Chinese inscription from the sixth century A.D.

Hephaestus crafting a weapon

for they went with two legs or four legs or six or any even number, but who ever heard of a creature with three?

Hephaestus refused to be spurned. He had a good brain. And strong hands and arms. And, most important of all, he was his mother's son. He would find a way to be powerful. He would show the others. He searched the Earth and came upon Lemnos, an island with a mountain that roared. The soft sand beaches felt like silk under his weary feet. The many trees offered shade at last. He bit into olives fat with oil and loved the way it dripped through his beard. He closed his eyes and delighted in the twittering calls of the little owls. He threw rocks into the fire of the volcano and watched them melt. Ah. This was a good place. The fire would give him all the power he needed.

Soon he'd made himself a hammer, an anvil, and a pair of tongs. He set to work making things—anything he wanted. Armor and helmets and chariots. Necklaces and drinking

cups and graceful little statues. Then he made himself a chair with wheels, so he could cross the land much faster. Everyone still poked fun at him, but they admired him all the same. They came asking him to invent things to meet their needs. He was generous and taught them how to craft things for themselves. Even Zeus came, and Hephaestus forged him a cape that served as his breastplate and came to be known as the Aegis—Zeus' symbol thereafter.

A sea nymph named Cabeiro fell in love with him, and they had two sons. Then he visited the island of Sicily, and the nymph Aetna fell in love with him and he fathered two more sons. Everywhere he went, someone loved him and someone bore him children.

But the one Hephaestus loved was Athena, the gray-eyed goddess who was the very cause of his existence. She liked to come and work beside him at the forge. She crafted things for household use, but what she excelled at was making anything to help in battle. She invented the bridle—clever girl. She made a soft twitter sound as she worked, almost like an owl in love. And she ate olives like a glutton. What more could he ask? For sure, she'd love him back—females did that.

But Athena had no interest in any man, least of all a lame one. She spurned Hephaestus' advances and left him seething.

Well, he'd show her, too. He'd get himself a wife that was the envy of the world. Just wait.

Hephaestus worked so hard to win the affections of Athena. He taught her to use the forge, where she perfected swords, shields, helmets, armor—everything to tickle a woman warrior's heart.

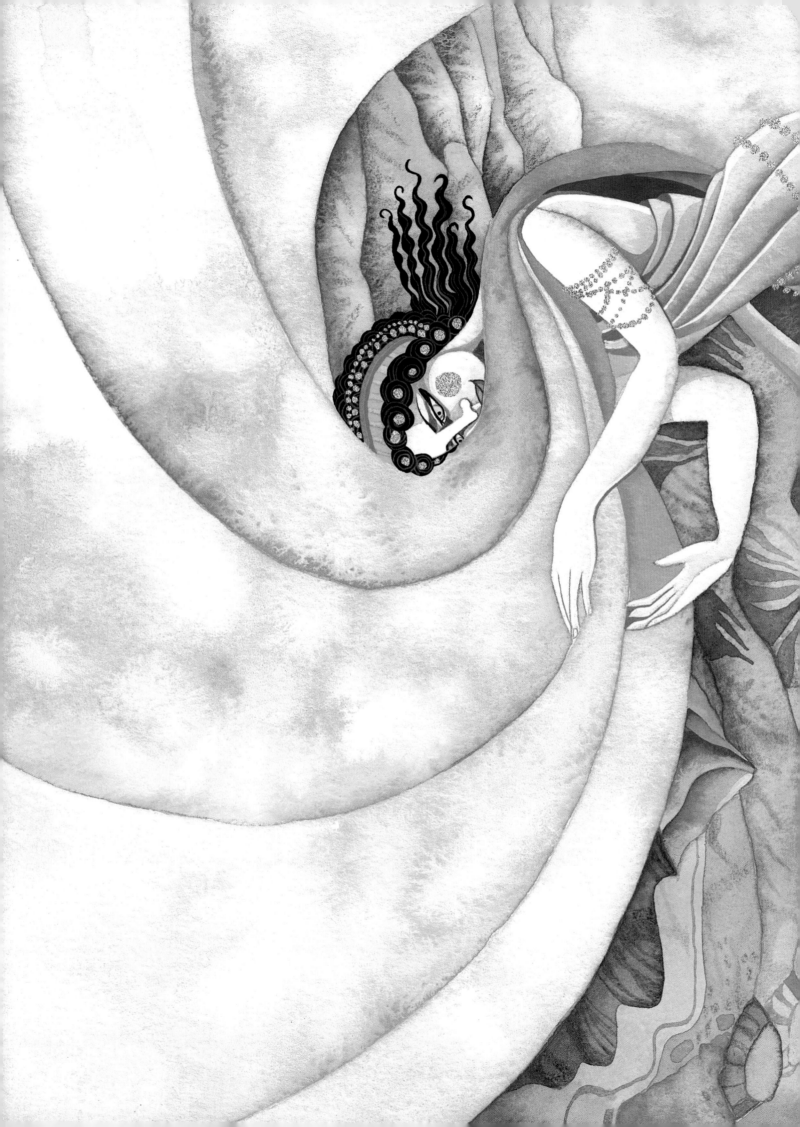

APHRODITE Goddess of Love & Beauty

APHRODITE
Goddess of Love & Beauty

When Cronus freed the Titans, he injured his father, Uranus, and hurled parts of him backward over his shoulder so that they scattered across the land and seas. Children sprang up, most from blood on the earth, but one from her father's foam mixing with sea foam: Aphrodite. Such a strange birth might not seem the most promising start in life, but this goddess was lovely from her first breath.

And she grew even lovelier. The changeable seas taught Aphrodite nuances of colors and movement, and she used them to inspire love. She could be almost transparent, then so richly hued a god felt he'd dined far too long but couldn't yet stop. She could touch a god like a cool welcome spray on a hot afternoon or slam him like a tsunami that threatened to never let him up for air. She perfected her charms, and all under the guidance of that ancient god, Eros, the one who first led Night into the arms of Erebus, and Gaia into the arms of Uranus. Eros considered Aphrodite his special project.

When Aphrodite was confident of her ability to enchant all the sea and river gods, she moved on to see how she'd fare with land gods. First, she went to the island of Cythera, then the island of Cyprus. Wherever her foot touched tender grasses sprouted and flowers bloomed, as though the ground itself felt blessed by her presence. And the gods… well, Aphrodite became a master at flirting in words and smiles and glances. She took up little deceits, flattering when necessary, teasing when effective. She never failed; if she wanted a god to love her, he did.

And the goddesses? They envied her at first. But Aphrodite didn't need every god everywhere to pine after her. So she taught the other divinities how to do what she did. And they practiced these feminine wiles well, but not quite as well as Aphrodite.

Which meant every god wanted her as his wife.

Zeus was alarmed. Discord among the gods could be dangerous. He had to step in and arrange a marriage for the gorgeous goddess quickly. But who? The husband of Aphrodite would be scorned by all others simply out of jealousy. Who could Zeus afford to have the others scorn?

STAR Light…Star Bright

Venus is the ancient Romans' name for Aphrodite. The planet Venus is the brightest object in the sky after the sun and the moon. Venus orbits the sun faster than Earth does. When it comes up "behind" Earth, it is visible after sunset. When it "overtakes" Earth, it is visible before sunrise. So it goes from being the Evening Star to being the Morning Star. The ancient Greeks were the first to recognize that these two "stars" were in fact one object.

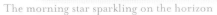

The morning star sparkling on the horizon

Then it was obvious: Everyone already scorned Hephaestus, the lame god of metalworking. Good. Nothing lost.

But it wasn't good for Aphrodite. Zeus was a thick-skulled idiot! She was the beauty of the universe, and she had honed her feminine skills so that she could marry any god she wanted. She'd be wasted on Hephaestus. The lame god was unsightly.

Aphrodite winced at the very thought of him.

Zeus wouldn't relent.

Hephaestus waited patiently through this debate, seeing immediately why Zeus had chosen him and, thus, knowing that the deal was sealed. He was overcome by the turn in his luck. Aphrodite was far better than the last wife he'd longed for, the goddess Athena, who had rejected him soundly and talked about nothing but war—why, she was battle-crazed. Aphrodite was totally unlike her. Hephaestus would make this marriage work. He would win Aphrodite's affections. He went to his forge and made her a gold belt with the most delicate and intricate filigree that anyone had ever seen. Only the slimmest needle could poke through the myriad loops.

Aphrodite took one look at the dazzling belt and donned it. She sensed instinctively that magic wove its way through the intrigues of the curlicues of that belt. Then she walked among the gods. Oh! Incomparable as Aphrodite was, this belt made her more so. She didn't have to whisper a word or bat an eye. Yes! With this girdle, Aphrodite could tolerate the marriage.

By crafting a glorious belt, Hephaestus finally won a wife, and what a wife—the glamorous Aphrodite. She couldn't resist the stunning belt; beauty will have beauty, after all.

HERMES Messenger of the Gods

HERMES
Messenger of the Gods

Zeus saw the nymph walking the Cyllene hills in the midst of sheep: Maia, daughter of Atlas. Clad in purple, she rose above the flock like an iris on a silvery stalk in a field of milkweed bolls. He wanted her as his wife. Which one would this be? He'd lost count. A cheery observation—the world teemed with lovely lasses.

His arms itched to hold her. But Hera, his queen, would surely learn of it. That would be unpleasant; Hera had become a royal nag.

So Zeus waited till evening and tucked Hera into bed, then snuck across the fragrant meadow and into the deep cave where Maia dwelled. The goddess turned her head in shyness so her thick curls covered her face. Zeus laughed loud; he could never resist the charms of sweet youth.

At dawn on the fourth day of the ninth month later, a perfect son leaped from Maia's womb into her arms. She named him Hermes and set him in a cradle deep within her cave home. But the tiny boy hopped out and ran for the mouth of the cave.

Hermes laughed in glee, the same way his father laughed the night he visited Maia. There in his path was a spangle-shelled tortoise. The boy killed it, then filled the emptied high-domed shell with cut reeds. He stretched ox hide over it, then used sheep horns to make a crosspiece and stretched seven gut strings upon them. Behold, this babe had just invented the first lyre. He strummed and sang to Maia; they spent the afternoon telling stories of the gods.

When Maia finally put Hermes into his cradle again and lounged upon her own bed, he waited for her to fall asleep—just as his father Zeus had waited for Hera to fall asleep the night he visited Maia. Then the babe crept from the cave. He followed the path of the waning sun to the shadowy mountains of Pieria, where he saw a herd of cattle, large and low-bellowing. These were Apollo's, the boy somehow knew. It pleased him to rob from such a stuck-up god.

He led away fifty cattle, magically reversing their hoof-prints so one would think they'd traveled the other direction. In a wooded spot, Hermes rubbed sticks together and invented fire and set a tree ablaze. He slew two long-horned cows and roasted them and offered their meat to the gods. Then he went stealthily into his mother's cave, moving like an autumn breeze. He climbed into his cradle and wrapped the swaddling cloth about his shoulders. But Maia awoke and sensed the trick immediately. She called him

TRICKSTER Tales

An illustration of Peter Pan

Crafty Hermes plays naughty baby tricks. Lots of mythological tricksters have babyish or animal ways. The British story of Peter Pan is about a boy who never grows up and plays all day. Many Native American stories tell of Coyote, a magical figure who gets involved in funny stories, but also often death stories. These tricksters do what they want, without thinking about the effects on others. We laugh, but we also see what a mess life would be if we all did that.

a knave. Hermes grinned. He vowed to steal whatever he wanted whenever he wanted.

When an older farmer told Apollo who had plundered his cattle, the god stomped to the sweet-smelling cave. In the cradle, Hermes pretended to be asleep. But Apollo demanded to know where the cattle were.

Hermes, all innocence, asked, "How could a newborn with feet soft as melted butter steal the cattle of the great Apollo? Imagine the public shame if it were true. But it's not."

Apollo stared, then burst out in laughter. "Crafty little liar. Lead me to my cattle."

"I swear I stole nothing!"

In a rage, Apollo picked up Hermes, who, as a baby will do, let out a trumpet blast from his bottom. Surprised, Apollo dropped him. But then he tucked him under an arm and carried him up Mount Olympus to demand a judgment from Zeus, the king of gods. Hermes still denied all. But Zeus saw through the deceit and told them, both his sons, to join forces and bring the cattle home.

Furious, Apollo tied Hermes up so he could steal no more. But the invincible babe broke through the ropes. Still, the timbre of Apollo's voice and the flash of his eyes finally convinced Hermes the problem wouldn't disappear on its own. Besides, Apollo was awesome in his anger, and Hermes wanted all the gods, but especially Apollo, to love

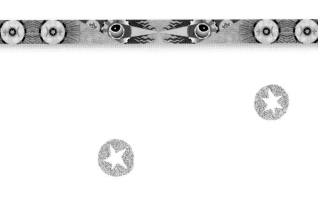

him. He took out his turtle-shell lyre and played so enchantingly flowers bent toward him. Then he gave the melody-dazed Apollo the lyre as a peace offering. Apollo played it so much better than Hermes that even rocks tumbled from precipices and rolled closer to the music.

The two half brothers vowed loyalty to one another, and Apollo gave Hermes three winged maidens—the Thriae, who could foretell the future—as a token of his friendship. In approval Zeus declared Hermes lord over birds of omen, as well as dogs, sheep, grim-eyed lions, and gleaming-tusked boars. And he appointed him messenger to Hades; Hephaestus forged him a helmet to make him invisible, like that of Hades, and sandals with wings, to help in his travels. But everyone still admitted the new god was a rogue.

A rogue. Spicy label. And it felt affectionate. The rogue smiled.

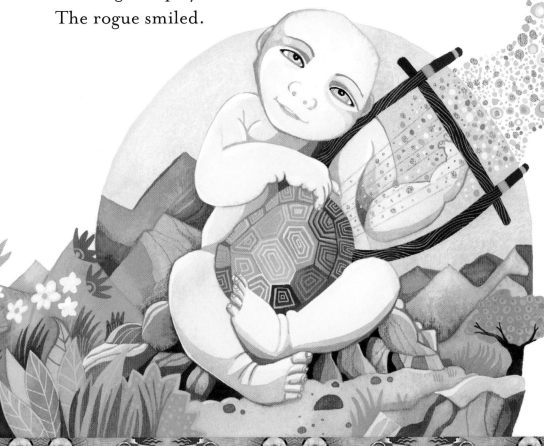

Hermes was born naughty, but also crafty. As a babe, he made the first lyre from a tortoise shell and sheep horn and guts. He played like a god.

ARES
God of War

At long last, the king of the gods, Zeus, and the queen of the gods, Hera, had a child together, a son they named Ares. This son should have been remarkable. After all, he was the first fully royal son. His parents put their hopes in him.

Ares swiftly disappointed both. He was strong enough, exceedingly strong, in fact. And highly skilled at driving a chariot and throwing a spear. But he used his talents to ill effect. He was murderous and cowardly at the same time, inciting strife and hatred. A stain upon the world, and a bloody one at that. His parents abhorred him.

But no one could deny he had a certain physical magnetism. He raced across the world with calves like iron, the swiftest of all the gods. His hands seemed capable of grabbing anything, anything at all, and holding tight. His squared-off jaw looked capable of crushing bone. His lips were full and peaked, and the thought of what they were capable of made goddesses tremble. His eyes dared others to meet them.

Aphrodite's eyes took the dare. Why shouldn't they? She was a goddess and a breathtaking beauty. The breathtaking beauty of the universe. And she was married to Hephaestus, a god certainly, but a blacksmith with a shriveled foot, who bent over a cauldron of molten metals all day long, coughing and wiping at his bleary, reddened eyes. He was ugly and growing uglier. She was willing to swear he limped more exaggeratedly each

GODS of War

Ares seems just plain nasty. Other gods of war in ancient cultures were likewise awful. Tyr, the god of war in Norse mythology, was also the god of strife; he went around causing trouble. Sekhmet, an ancient Egyptian goddess of war, loved bloodshed. When a war ended, the people had to give her a big celebration in order to soothe her, otherwise she would have continued killing until everyone was dead. War gods seemed to have in common a frenzy for destruction.

An ancient mural painting of the fierce Egyptian goddess, Sekhmet

day. So it was her right to flirt with Ares.

Which she did. She and Ares did whatever they wanted right there in Hephaestus' home, while the old god was out at his forge. They figured he'd never know.

But Helios, the sun god who was the child of Titans, saw them through the window. He liked Hephaestus; the two of them worked with fire and this gave them a special bond. He told.

Hephaestus couldn't claim surprise. He'd always known it would be hard to hold on to his glorious wife. But the open wound seared. He had to take action. In a duel of brawn, he'd lose. So it had to be a duel of brains.

He set his great anvil upon its stand and hammered. He hammered all the rest of the day, all night long, all the next day, until the pile of thin metal loops stood taller than he was. Then he hammered them together into a metal net so fine it was as hard to see as a spiderweb, but it was strong—strong enough for the task. The following day, when Ares and

ARES

Aphrodite were resting, Hephaestus spread a metal net over the two of them. When they woke, they found themselves ensnared.

Hephaestus quickly called together all the gods to come view the pair. The goddesses didn't come, but every male god did, jeering and laughing, ready to stand in judgment.

Hephaestus had done it—the weaker god, the ugly god, he'd prevailed over mighty Ares. The gods were quick to congratulate him, quick to celebrate that right had won over evil.

But then the gods looked at Aphrodite in all her stunning grace and felt instantly dizzy. Hermes turned to Apollo and asked what he wouldn't give to be the one caught in that net with Aphrodite rather than Ares. It was a joke, but the arrow hit home. No one could blame Ares. And how could anyone place blame on that vision of loveliness, Aphrodite? Thus the two lovers went unpunished.

Embarrassed, Aphrodite fled to Cyprus, where she let her nymphs comfort her with perfumes and warm baths.

Ares felt more annoyance than anything else. In their

> Aphrodite betrayed her husband; Ares betrayed his brother. Hephaestus got the better of them: He trapped them in a metal net and held them up for public shame.

time together, Aphrodite had borne him children, two of whom, Phobos and Deimos, accompanied him in his sackings and onslaughts. But who needed the trouble of her when she came with that madman of a husband? So he went on to other loves. And other hates. He was the god of war—what else is there to say?

HELIOS Sun God

HELIOS
Sun God

All the while that the ancestral line of the Titan Cronus was growing, the ancestral lines of the other Titans were also growing. Upon being freed from the hollows of their mother Gaia, the Titans had scattered widely across the waters and the lands. And two of them, Hyperion and Theia, had taken to the skies. Hyperion hovered above like a gauzy blanket of the clearest blue, and Theia pierced through him in points of startling light. She was the shining eyes of the universe, the brilliant jewels of the skies.

It wasn't long before they had three children: Helios, the sun; Selene, the moon; and then, their natural companion, Eos, the dawn.

Helios was born tireless and good-natured. He rose each day without fail and put on his golden helmet and yoked together his mighty stallions to a golden chariot that the god Hephaestus had made just for him. He rode it high, so very high, across the skies. All anyone below could see of him was a ball of light so bright it dazzled, with streaks following behind—his streaming locks and fluttering garments. Strong rays beamed from him; they penetrated all but the most closed crevices of the Earth. Helios watched what happened to the other gods when he was present; they absorbed his heat, earth and water and air gods alike. They felt more expansive, more relaxed. They smiled more; they did small kindnesses for each other. Helios spread comfort. What a privilege! The realization made him stand taller.

Daily he rose to the highest point of the heavens, lingered there, then continued on until he plunged into the waters in the far west and yielded the sky to his sister Selene. It took him all night to make his way quietly back to the east, then he began the long journey all over again. But never, not even for a moment, did it occur to him to take a break for a while. Others needed him simply to maintain their sanity. Helios was, beyond all else, reliable.

That's what caught the attention of Prometheus, whose father was a Titan and whose mother was the daughter of a Titan: Helios was a constant. It got Prometheus thinking. One could count on a rhythm to the universe, a certain heat, a unifying force. He was digging in the clay and silt and sand by a briny river delta one day, noticing how he could smear the wet mixture on his arms and Helios would dry it so stiff that it became like a shell, but thin, a second skin—a second skin!—and the thought

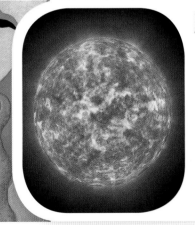

LIFE-GIVING Sun

In Greek mythology, humans appear at one point with no discussion of how they were created. But in later Roman myths, especially by Ovid, Prometheus creates humans. Today we know the sun was crucial to the creation of all life on Earth. For that reason, Helios was woven into the creation of humanity in this story. But the ancients may well have seen no connection between the sun and life on Earth.

A photograph of the sun in space

possessed him; an outrageous idea, really. He could form something from this clay, something in his own image, in the image of a god. Helios would bake it until it held together, and every day he'd bake it anew and keep it whole.

Prometheus and Helios fashioned humans out of clay. But the idea of creating mortals in their own image delighted the gods, and more and more of them added what they could.

And Helios agreed. Why not? Gods were superb, after all. What could be better than clay figures just like them? In fact, with just a little energy, these figures could come to life. They wouldn't last forever, of course. But they'd be interesting toys, however briefly they breathed.

And so Prometheus fashioned the new creatures and called them men. The other gods looked on with interest. Soon Hephaestus, the smithy god, joined in the endeavor and, encouraged by Zeus, fashioned women. Athena, the goddess who sprang from Zeus' forehead, taught the women to weave. Aphrodite, the goddess who emerged from the sea foam, taught the women how to flirt. And Hermes, son of Zeus and Maia, taught the women to deceive.

And all these men and women were held together, body and soul, by Helios. He liked these simple creatures. He set an oak tree on fire so they could take sticks and carry the fire with them wherever they wanted and warm themselves as they huddled together.

SELENE
Goddess of the Moon

Selene was the second child of the Titans Hyperion and Theia, and the sister to the sun god Helios and the dawn goddess Eos. Her brother was not a show-off, but he wasn't retiring, either. He did the world a magnificent service, giving a regularity to life with his daily travel across the sky, and he accepted the deserved praise he received. He fathered many, all with radiant eyes. Eos, likewise, put herself forth, without being the least bit gaudy. She announced her brother's arrival every day by stretching her rosy fingers to the eastern sky. The very sight of her gave hope, so she was easy to fall in love with. Astraios, the son of Titans, mingled with her and they produced the stars and the three winds: Zephyr, who came from the west and lightly cleared the skies; Boreas, who struck swiftly and chillingly from the north; and Notos, the storm-bringer from the south, who rumbled through in late summer and early autumn.

But Selene differed from her siblings. Her shyness was painful. Sometimes her compulsion to close in upon herself was like a bear in winter. She couldn't fight it. She hid completely. Then she'd hear the wails. She'd cover her ears, but they penetrated through her long-winged fingers, through her rich tresses. And she couldn't deny the women—they needed her. They were calling her back so piteously. And she'd come, she'd reveal herself again, little by little,

STAR LIGHT Star Bright

The ancient Greeks grouped star clusters into constellations named after humans, animals, and other things. Wandering "stars" had god or goddess names. Today we know that the stars in a constellation are not related in any particular way. Their apparent closeness is a line-of-sight effect. Further, wandering "stars" are planets, the sun (Helios), or the moon (Selene). Until modern times, many people relied on astrology—study of the celestial bodies—for omens when making decisions. The sun and the moon were considered the most important astrologically.

A photograph of the moon

offering the comfort of a soft light that allowed them to make their way in merciful obscurity. Over two weeks she'd wax fuller and fuller, until, gibbous and magnificent, she gleamed over mountain peaks, glistened over waves. She bathed sweethearts with such tenderness they were never quite sure how it happened, but somehow, in some blessedly peaceful way, they realized they'd found the right person at last, their soul mate at long last. They found calm. All because of Selene.

And then, so predictably, they'd sing to her, serenade her, make her flush with their hyperboles, their obviousness, until she had to pull back, shrink again, wane and wane and disappear. Only the most discerning could detect the filmy trace of her, the knife edge outline in the blackest sky.

For a little while she felt safe. Then the wails began again. The cycle started anew. Helios brought a daily rhythm that all humans marched to, but Selene brought a monthly rhythm that

pulsed inside women and gave them the power to be mothers. They wailed and wailed for this most transfixing of powers.

One night Selene shone down on a man, a human, asleep in the open. She moved closer. He woke and looked her full in the face and said nothing for the longest time. Then he whispered, details of a heart she admired the more she learned of it. His quiet beauty dumbfounded her. Humans were mere toys to the other

Selene was the first deity to love a human. Mortal with immortal—a doomed love. But Zeus put Endymion in an endless sleep so he wouldn't age and die. Sad solution.

gods, but Selene saw substance; she touched this man's spirit and realized she had found her own soul mate, at last.

The revelation hurt. Endymion was mortal; he would age and die. Selene pushed the thought aside and let herself love and be loved. But the passing of time only made their love grow until the idea of ever being unable to look upon Endymion's perfect face made Selene's heart crumple. She begged Zeus to help her, to keep Endymion as he was, forever. Zeus responded by putting the man into an eternal sleep—a solution that gave Selene that undeniable sadness that poets have sung of ever since.

Selene and Endymion had fifty daughters, called the Menae, who took turns accompanying their mother each night.

Selene, silver sweet, and soft, and sad.

DIONYSUS
God of Wine

There she was again: Semele. Zeus' mouth watered. But Semele was human. He followed, intoxicated by her beauty. Mortal mortal—did it matter?

The moon goddess Selene's love of the human Endymion had incited a spate of such unions. But Zeus was the king of gods. It would be humiliation to have a child that grew old and feeble, lost teeth, hair, sight, hearing.

Still, that girl, that little snip of a mortal girl, ooh, he loved that girl. Ha! Zeus would simply make any child that came of this union immortal. Ha ha! He instantly declared himself to her.

Semele, daughter of King Cadmus of Thebes, was just as instantly enthralled.

Bang! Zeus had another wife. And, against expectations, something about Semele got to him. The blueness of her veins, the dark circles that formed under her eyes when she'd missed a night's sleep because of cavorting with him, the strange sour-sweet of her meat-eating breath. She wouldn't last. The heart of the king was actually touched. He swore he'd grant her any wish.

Boom! Hera went ballistic. She visited Semele, all sisterly and loving. "Isn't Zeus astonishing? If only he'd let you see him in full splendor as Lord of the Thunderbolt. That would make you truly understand who he is."

Semele was sweet and pretty but far from bright; she asked Zeus to come to her in bursting glory.

Zeus knew what the outcome would be. He begged Semele to change her mind, but she wouldn't believe the danger. Alas, he had to honor his promise. Trapped in a melodrama, he granted her wish.

Semele burst into flames.

The distraught god snatched the baby inside her and nestled him in his own thigh until birth. Then Zeus traveled to the valley of Nysa, and there the nymphs raised his divine son, Dionysus.

Dionysus taught farmers to grow vines, pick their grapes according to the autumn stars, hold them a fortnight for further ripening, then press them into wine stored in earthen jars. The wine flowed like a deep purple river, and the farmers drank gratefully, toasting the generosity of Dionysus.

One day pirates saw the young god on shore. They judged him a prince from his clothing, so they dragged him aboard for ransom. They went to tie him to the mast, but the ropes

Clusters of grapes hanging from a vine

THE GIVING Grape

Dionysus is the god of wine. Wine originated in the Caucasus and Iran. It appeared in Greece around 4500 B.C. Greece is rocky, so olive trees grow easily. Though there is little soil soft enough to be plowed, Greece's climate helps.

For many months it's dry and sunny, then it's humid and cool (typically mild, but it can snow in the mountains). Greeks quickly learned to grow grapes on sunny terraces and make wine. They taught these arts to the rest of Europe.

fell away. The helmsman guessed he was a god. But the crew didn't listen. With one breath from Dionysus, the sails filled, and perfumed wine streamed across the ship deck. The crew finally understood, but before they could put Dionysus back on land, he changed into a lion and charged. They jumped overboard and became dolphins forever after.

Such were the two sides of Dionysus: graceful and jarring, clear and filthy, bliss-bearing and tormenting. He brought men some of the most carefree moments of their lives, and he brought men to despondency.

But it was women he most affected. He excited them to frenzy. Some abandoned their children to follow him. Pentheus, King of Thebes, didn't believe Dionysus was a god. He put him in prison. But Dionysus broke out and crazed the women of Thebes so they came with him. When Pentheus followed, Dionysus robbed the women of their senses completely, so that they attacked him—his mother among them. They ripped Pentheus limb from limb. Then Dionysus freed them from their insanity, and they saw what they had done. Wicked tragedy.

Dionysus traveled in a chariot bearing the most delicious harvest of his vines, but pulled by panthers. The message was clear: Beware, beware.

Dionysus was changeable—from calm and sweet to wild and hateful. Here his rage at being disrespected transformed him into a lion. The frightened crew dove overboard and became dolphins.

PERSEUS
The Ill-Fated Hero

The wife of Acrisius, king of the city of Argos, gave birth to a beautiful daughter, Danaë, but what the king wanted was a son. So he traveled to the temple at Delphi, where the priestess told reliable prophecies—she was the most revered oracle of all Greece. The oracle said not only would Acrisius never father a son, but that the son of his daughter would kill him.

Acrisius wouldn't harm the girl for fear of retribution from the gods. So he promptly had a bronze home built for her underground, with an opening to the sky for air and light. Hour after hour, day after day, year after year, the poor prisoner sat on the ground of that opening with her face turned to the heavens. She became a lover of sunlight and moonlight, of wind and rain.

Zeus spied the sweetheart face and instantly sensed what would delight her most and so came to her as a golden downpour. Soon Danaë had a son, Perseus. Acrisius again moved promptly. He put daughter and babe into a wooden box and set them to sea.

Danaë wrapped her beloved son in her cloak and bade him sleep, sleep. She cooed, her mouth to his ear, as the wild waters rocked them, and her wild heart cried. Please, let no hideous watery creature slither up from underneath and snatch them, or open wide its gigantic jaws and swallow them.

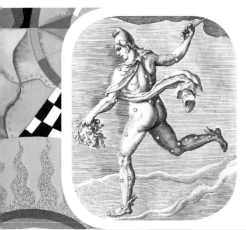

CONSTELLATION Perseus

Among the largest northern sky constellations is Perseus, visible in winter, especially December. It contains "double stars." Some are simply lined up to appear close to each other but really are far apart. Others are "binary," so close they are caught in each other's gravity, in mutual orbit. It also contains "variable stars." For some, brightness varies because they swell and shrink. For others, brightness varies because of an orbiting star that eclipses them.

An illustration of the constellation Perseus

The box washed ashore on the island Seriphos, where a fisherman took care of them and raised the boy. Perseus grew strong, but he never lost his sense of wariness. His mother and he had survived his grandfather's perfidy, but the world was dangerous. He trod forth, courageous, yes, but with eyes darting, on the lookout.

Over the years the king of the island, Polydectes, fell in love with Danaë, but she refused him. Perseus, adult now, sensed something dishonorable in the man. So he protected his mother from the king's advances.

Polydectes felt affronted. What? Perseus dared to thwart a king? In the selfish tradition so common of kings, he chose to simply get rid of the youth, just as King Acrisius had.

He threw a party to which guests were supposed to bring

horses as gifts, so that he could, he said, use them as a proper marriage offer in his quest for the hand of another young woman who tamed horses. Perseus was delighted that Polydectes would marry and thus leave his mother alone. He promised Polydectes any gift he wanted, even the head of the Gorgon Medusa, wife of the sea god Poseidon. The rash words came out of nowhere, but there they were, glittering in the air, and Polydectes grabbed them with triumph.

Medusa had serpents for hair, and anyone who looked upon her instantly turned to stone. As far as Polydectes was concerned, Perseus was history.

The three Graeae shared one eye and one tooth. Perseus ransomed that eye and that tooth for knowledge that allowed him to kill the Graeae's sister. Clever, no? But heartless.

But Perseus was Zeus' son, and two of his siblings came to his rescue. First was the goddess Athena; she told Perseus that three nymphs, the Hesperides, had the weapons to kill Medusa. But to find out where the Hesperides were, Perseus had to ask the three Graeae. The Graeae were sisters of Medusa. They had been born as old women, with but a single eye and a single tooth to share among them. Perseus hid and watched them huddling like three huge gray birds. As one woman passed the eye and tooth to another, he snatched both and demanded they lead him to the garden of the Hesperides. It was a terrible ransom; their sister would die if they answered, they would deprive themselves of sight and food if they didn't. The Graeae led him there, and Perseus gave back the eye and tooth.

The Hesperides lent Perseus three things: winged sandals like those of the god Hermes so that he could fly, the helmet of invisibility that had belonged to the god Poseidon, and a wallet that could contain anything without getting larger. To these Athena added a bronze shield so bright it reflected like a mirror. And now the god Hermes finally joined the quest; he gave Perseus an adamantine sickle.

Perseus, newly invisible and armed, flew to the cave where Medusa slept with her two sisters. He stood over them in their sleep and held the polished shield up by his

shoulder so he could look into it to see their reflection. Never had he imagined such ugliness. Their serpent hair coiled around them, making their whole bodies seem scaly. Long sharp porcine tusks protruded from their lower jaws. Gold wings sprouted from their backs, and their hands were bronze. The god Poseidon called Medusa his jewel, yet how he could bear being near her was beyond Perseus.

With one powerful slice, the youth cut off Medusa's head. From her neck sprang full grown the children that Poseidon had fathered. One was Pegasus, a winged horse, who eventually made his way to Olympus. The other was Chrysaor, a huge warrior with a gold sword, who became the king of all Iberia. Perseus allowed the two to flee, as he put Medusa's head into the wallet, then flew away. The two Gorgon sisters of Medusa cried out. They wanted to give chase, but Perseus was invisible.

He flew over water along the north coast of Africa, heading home, when he saw a maiden tied to a rock jutting out of the sea. Perseus flew to her and she told him her story.

Andromeda was the daughter of King Cepheus and his bride Cassiopeia, both of whom loved to walk along the shore and show off how handsome they were. But Cassiopeia lacked sense. She boasted that her beauty surpassed that of the sea nymphs, the Nereids. Gods and goddesses took challenges even less well than human royalty did. The Nereids complained to the sea god Poseidon,

Perseus used his shield as a mirror to see Medusa's head so he could slay her without danger to himself. Clever again, heartless again. Medusa had done him no wrong.

who sent a tsunami and a monstrous hungry whale to ravage the land. But King Cepheus had heard the prophecy that calamity could be avoided if he sacrificed his daughter to the whale. So there she was—Andromeda, quaking on the boulder. Her eyes burned as they scanned the horizon for her coming death.

The winds whipped the girl's hair so that it seemed to fly around her. Her bottom lip trembled. Her fingers curled around each other, bluish in fear. Her heart thumped so hard, Perseus heard it, and his heart beat even harder. Saving this pretty pretty maid from being eaten would be even better than saving his mother from the nasty king.

And here came the whale. But it wasn't a whale at all, it was a giant scaly serpent, rising on a tide taller than the tallest tree. The monster seemed borne of the nightmares the babe Perseus had seen in that wooden box at the mercy of the terrifying sea. But he could do this. Perseus told King Cepheus he would kill the sea monster if the king would give his daughter to him in marriage. The king agreed, of course, and Perseus slew the dragon, whose dying cry deafened the seabirds as far as one could see and whose blood

Lovely Andromeda was to be sacrificed to a sea monster because of her parents' foolish boasts. But when the monster came, Perseus attacked. Classic maiden in distress; classic hero.

turned the entire ocean red.

At long last, Perseus found his way home and turned to stone King Polydectes and the friends he'd gathered around him. Then he gave Medusa's head to Athena, who attached it to the center of her shield. And he gave the winged sandals, the helmet of invisibility, and the now empty wallet to Hermes to return to the Hesperides as promised.

Eventually Perseus, Andromeda, and Perseus' mother Danaë decided to go to Argos to see Danaë's parents. But when Danaë's father Acrisius heard they were coming, he snuck away to the land of the Pelasgians. As luck would have it, the king there was hosting an athletic contest, and he invited Perseus to take part. In the competitions, Perseus threw his discus, and it hit Acrisius in the foot, killing him instantly. Pure accident. Ill-fated Perseus had unwittingly fulfilled the oracle's prediction.

ORION
The Hunter

The sea god Poseidon and the Gorgon Medusa wrapped each other in tenderness. Each was the precious stone at the center of the other's being. Looking at him with his fearsome trident and her with those thrashing snakes coming out of her head, it wasn't the sort of thing anyone could have guessed, but there it was. Love.

Then the youth Perseus appeared out of nowhere and for no reason cut off Medusa's head, as one might slaughter a monster. If Perseus hadn't been the son of Zeus, Poseidon might have sought revenge. What a sad event. The only good thing was that Poseidon and Medusa's two unborn children escaped: the huge warrior Chrysaor and the winged horse Pegasus.

In his grief, Poseidon fell into the arms of Medusa's sister, the Gorgon Euryale. From their mingling came a son, Orion. Poseidon was overjoyed to have a child, not a giant or a horse. He spoiled the boy rotten, and when Orion became a man, Poseidon gave him a gift: the ability to walk on water.

It was too much, really, walking on water; it fed the youth's arrogance. Orion grew into an insufferably pompous nitwit. His wife Side was equally pompous and dimwitted, for she claimed to rival the goddess Hera in beauty. Hera grabbed the girl and cast her into Tartarus; that was the end of Orion's first marriage.

Undaunted, Orion went to the island of Chios to seek the hand of Merope, daughter to King Oenopion, known for her delicate face. Merope liked Orion. He was handsome and so good an archer he cleared the island of wild beasts at her behest. But the king took an immediate dislike to this swaggering braggart and called upon Dionysus, the god of wine, to help get rid of Orion.

Dionysus came and put on a party with dancing women—the Maenads—and enchanting music, savory foods, generous wine. Orion thoroughly enjoyed himself, so much so that he woke up in the morning on the seashore. How did he get there? And he was blinded! And now, yes, he remembered the king yelling at him, but for what? Had he offended someone? But this was a terrible thing for a king to do to his guest, no matter what the offense. Now Orion's outrage flamed; he would have revenge!

He stumbled to the forge of Hephaestus and lifted one of the smithy god's helpers onto his shoulders. He told him to guide his path to the island of Lemnos, where the sun rose.

HUNTER in the Sky

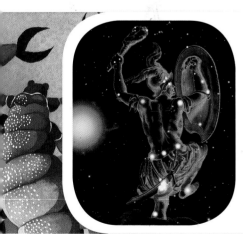

The belt of sky that circles the Earth above the Equator is the celestial Equator. The constellation Orion sits there, and it can be viewed from anywhere in the world, in any season. Three bright stars form a slanted line that is the hunter's belt. Four bright stars seem to mark the corners of a tall box, and they are the outer edges of the hunter's body. These seven stars make Orion one of the most noticeable and easily recognized constellations in the night sky.

An illustration of the constellation Orion

Orion stood there, still as a stone. Eos, the rosy goddess of the dawn, looked down and interpreted the determination in the man's stance as hope. Sympathy made her dip her face from the heavens and kiss his eyelids. Orion's sight was restored. Eos now shivered with love.

Orion pulled back from Eos' embrace. He wanted only to punish King Oenopion. The king heard Orion was coming and fled. Merope held no interest for him anymore, so Orion wandered, while poor Eos pined for him.

It was on Delos that Orion met the goddess Artemis and became her hunting companion. Artemis had never known anyone with archery skill that rivaled her own. They challenged each other, picking targets farther and farther away. The goddess was drawn to the muscular man in ways that confused her. She had never longed for a husband, but now she felt the stirrings of that strange thing—love.

Apollo, her brother, watched the developing romance with distaste. He liked his sister just the way she was—a maiden interested in the world of nature. If she changed, who knew how meddlesome she might become?

So Apollo tricked Artemis. He knew that Orion went by two names, the other being Candaon. And he knew that Artemis was unaware of Orion's other name. Now it just happened that there was another man named Candaon, who was a nasty fellow by anyone's reckoning. That other Candaon was hated by Artemis because he had been brutal to one of her followers.

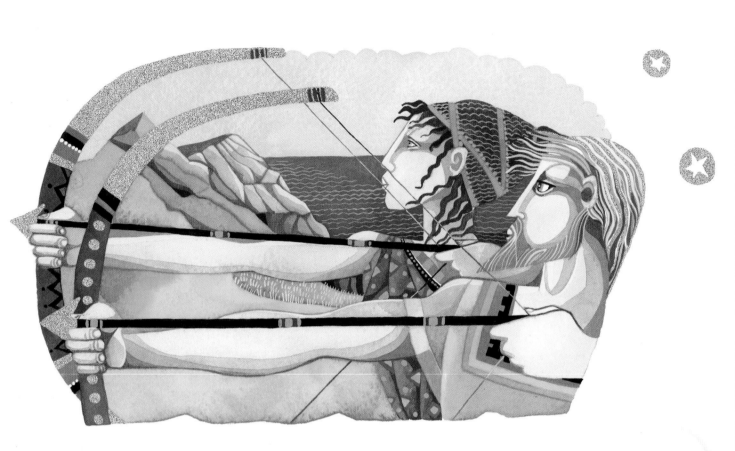

One day when Orion was swimming, Apollo pointed at him and told Artemis that there, far out in the sea, was the wicked Candaon. In anger, Artemis aimed her arrow at the distant figure. Then she swam out and fetched the body.

Woe! Hideous and hateful brother, who had made her kill the only man she'd ever loved. Wretched trick, wretched goddess, wretched world. Artemis and her mother Leto appealed to her father, the god Zeus, who placed Orion in the heavens as a constellation.

Orion went through life almost haphazardly, showing little care for others. In his eternal spot in the skies, he stayed true to that nature. Artemis, still enamored, waved to him often. Orion enjoyed the admiration his fixed pose drew, but he never waved back.

Elusive Artemis, the greatest archer, found a match in the human Orion. Nothing could have been more seductive. This was her only romance. Alas that it ended in bitter tragedy.

HERACLES *
The Hero Who Became Immortal

Amphitryon, king of Troezen, was a fierce general. He brought his wife Alcmena with him while he engaged in battle. Zeus, the king of gods, noticed her beauty. That she was already married was a pesky problem, however. So Zeus disguised himself as Amphitryon. Nine months later she gave birth to two boys: Iphicles, son of Amphitryon, and Heracles, son of Zeus. Alcmena had no idea the boys were anything but natural twins.

As soon as Hera, Zeus' queen wife, found out about this new wife, she flew into her usual fury. She decided to torment Zeus and Alcmena's child. Even before Heracles was born, Hera began her campaign against him. At the time, the woman Nicippe was also with child—she was to bear Eurystheus. The two unborn babes, Heracles and Eurystheus, were cousins since they shared Perseus as their grandfather. Whichever boy was born first would become the local king. So Hera delayed Heracles' birth by tying Alcmena's legs in knots, until his cousin Eurystheus could be born.

But that wasn't enough to placate her for long. She watched the baby Heracles and her heart grew ever more bitter. So she attacked. When Heracles and his half brother Iphicles were eight months old, asleep in their crib, two gigantic snakes slithered into their room and flicked their

*Greek gods and goddesses also have Roman names. Greek heroes, however, have only one name. The exception is Heracles, better known by his Roman name Hercules.

forked tongues across the boys' cheeks. Iphicles screamed. But Heracles grabbed each snake around the throat. Alcmena and Amphitryon came rushing to find Iphicles in tears but Heracles laughing with the limp snakes hanging from his fists. Hera bit her own fists in frustration.

The parents bowed in astonishment. Such a special child merited an education, so a series of tutors came. The music tutor made the mistake of striking Heracles for not playing right. The boy exploded with temper and smashed a lute over his head, killing him. It was unintended; Heracles didn't understand his strength yet. He couldn't have been more sorry.

But Amphitryon, fearing that Heracles might unwittingly do more harm, sent the boy to grow up among the cattle herds. A ferocious lion made the mistake of preying in just that area. At only 18, the youth went to hunt the lion. He strangled it with his bare hands, dressed in its skin, and put its gaping mouth over his head like a helmet.

BRAWN vs. Brain

Heracles engaged in a fight with the centaur Nessus

Heracles was the most famous hero of a particular type in ancient Greece: He was strong, confident, and courageous. But he was also either thoughtless or dense. He solved problems with brawn, not brain; he slew person after person, army after army, monster after monster. He made mistakes and felt awful about them, but he never changed his ways, he never learned from his mistakes. Yet at times he seemed almost jolly. The Greeks revered him, but they laughed at him, too.

On his way home, Heracles came across heralds from King Erginus of the Minyans. They were going to Thebes to collect an annual tribute of a hundred cattle as settlement for a past dispute. The men made the mistake of disparaging Thebes, Heracles' birthplace. In a rage, Heracles cut off their ears, noses, and hands. When Erginus responded with war on Thebes, Heracles led the Theban army to victory.

By now word had gotten around not to make the mistake of crossing Heracles. But bloodshed still lay ahead. The king of Thebes wed his daughter Megara to Heracles. They had three sons. Hera's jealousy boiled again. She afflicted Heracles with a sudden madness. He threw his sons and two nephews into a fire. When the madness passed, Heracles was horrified; self-loathing filled him. In self-imposed exile, he fled to the temple at Delphi.

The Delphic oracle told him to go to Tiryns, one of three Mycenaean cities, where the king would give him a list of ten labors. Once he had done these, his sins would be forgiven and he would be immortal. What Heracles didn't know was that King Eurystheus was guided by Hera.

Heracles' first labor was to kill the Nemean lion that terrorized the countryside. Heracles' arrows bounced off the beast. So Heracles chased it with raised club into a cave, where he strangled it. Then he carried the pelt back to

Mycenae. Eurystheus gaped at this proof of the incomparable strength and fearlessness of Heracles. After that he wouldn't allow Heracles into the city but gave all orders from afar.

The second labor was to kill the Lernaean Hydra, a swamp monster with nine heads, of which the center one was immortal. Heracles wrestled the Hydra to the ground. Each time he struck a head off with his club, two new heads sprouted. Worse, the Hydra called a colossal crab to come bite Heracles' foot. Heracles crushed the crab and called upon his nephew Iolaos for help. Iolaos brought a burning firebrand. Now when Heracles cut off a head, he quickly seared the neck so nothing could grow from it. Finally, he cut off the last head and buried it under a boulder. Then he dipped his arrows into the bitter bile inside the Hydra's liver to make them poisonous. King Eurystheus shook his head at the news. Because Heracles had been aided by his nephew this labor didn't count. He'd have to do an eleventh!

Heracles' second labor on his road to purification was to slay the Hydra, whose nine heads came at him simultaneously. Each time he sliced off a head, another two grew.

The third labor was to capture the Cerynitian hind, an elegant doe with golden horns loved by the goddess Artemis. Heracles chased the hind for a year before he wounded it lightly as it crossed a stream, then carried it to Mycenae alive. The fourth labor was to capture the Erymanthian boar, which Heracles did by chasing it into deep snow and noosing it. The fifth labor was to clean out the dung from the stables of the cattle of Augeias in one day. Heracles did it, but demanded pay from Augeias. King Eurystheus again refused to count this labor since it had been done for pay. So now Heracles had to do a twelfth! The sixth labor was to drive away the Stymphalian birds, which people feared would attract wolves. Heracles frightened the flock with castanets, then shot them with arrows as they flew away. The seventh labor was to fetch the famous wild bull of Crete, which he promptly did. The eighth labor was to bring back the man-eating mares of King Diomedes in Thrace. Heracles had to fight Diomedes' army and kill the king first, but he succeeded.

The ninth labor was to fetch the belt of Hippolyte, the queen of the Amazons, the tenth to fetch the cattle of Geryon

from Erytheia, the eleventh to fetch golden apples from the tree guarded by the Hesperides nymphs, and the twelfth to fetch the dog Cerberus from Hades. To Heracles each labor of fetching seemed more difficult than the last, and in fact, it was, because the goddess Hera put obstacles in his way. Heracles had to fight centaurs—unruly creatures, man from the chest up, but horses below—kill a sea monster about to devour a young woman, kill robbers, wrestle with all manner of other challengers. But he never lagged.

Finally, Heracles' spirit was pure, but only for a short time. Heracles passed his life getting caught up in situations where his anger made him violent and then repenting at length.

He married again—Deianeira, daughter of the king of Calydon. They traveled to a dangerous river. Heracles crossed on his own. But he paid the centaur Nessus to ferry his wife across. Nessus hated Heracles, for he had been among the centaurs that Heracles fought during his years of labor. The centaur threw himself upon Deianeira. Heracles shot Nessus with one of his arrows dipped in poisonous Hydra blood. As the centaur was dying, he told Deianeira that if she ever needed a love

Heracles' labors made him battle strange, vicious creatures. Perhaps the most terrifying was Cerberus, the three-headed hound who guarded the entrance to the Underworld and kept those imprisoned there from escaping.

potion to use on Heracles, his blood would work. Deianeira believed him—who knows why—and kept the centaur's poisoned blood in a vial. It would prove to be Heracles' doom.

But Heracles wasn't only doom and gloom. He ate and drank as much as a dozen men, and he enjoyed parties. And, most of all, he had a sense of humor. Once two rowdy fellows stole his bow, and Heracles hung them from a yoke across his neck. As they dangled there, they noticed he had a hairy bottom and poked fun. Their joking was infectious; Heracles laughed and set them free.

And Heracles had moments of true heroism. Once he arrived at the home of King Admetos in Thessaly. The king set him to eat alone, but Heracles realized that the household was crying. The king's wife, Alcestis, had just died. It was a terrible story, because the goddess Artemis had demanded that Admetos die for an earlier offense, but he could live if another died willingly in his place. Admetos' parents refused. But his wife Alcestis sacrificed herself, kissing their children goodbye. Heracles went to Tartarus and fought the god Hades and brought back Alcestis to Admetos, thus setting right a tale that was otherwise so wrong.

Still, Heracles' ending was insanely painful. His wife Deianeira worried that his love for her was waning. So she gave him a cloak soaked with the centaur's blood—blood tainted with the venomous Hydra's blood. Heracles put on the cloak and writhed and screamed as the poison ate into him. It hurt so horribly that he

built a pyre for himself and climbed on. Then he gave his bow and arrows to a young follower, Philoctetes, and convinced him to set the pyre aflame. Heracles burned up.

The cloud of his body rose to the heavens, where he was accepted as one of the immortals. And, in one of the strangest turns of the heart, his nemesis Hera not only received him with grace, but gave him one of her daughters in marriage. Perhaps that was Heracles' fate from the start, since his name meant "glory of Hera."

Ravaged by the pain of poison, Heracles built a pyre and immolated himself. But first, and fatefully (as we shall see), he gave his friend Philoctetes his bow and arrows.

JASON Wanderer of the Seas

JASON
Wanderer of the Seas

An oracle told King Pelias of Iolcus to beware of a man wearing one sandal. The king had reason to worry at this oracle. He had seized the throne from his half brother Aeson and killed all of Aeson's children. Any man who had done such a thing certainly couldn't relax. After all, a dishonorable soul always expects the worst.

In fact, Aeson's wife, Alcimede, was with child when King Pelias killed the rest of her family. She pretended that the new baby was stillborn and secretly sent the boy, Jason, away to be raised safely and educated well by the only decent centaur, Chiron. Chiron did his job admirably; he trained Jason in the hunt, the arts, and nature.

When Jason was grown and ready to claim the throne that was rightfully his, he set out to return to his birthplace. With each step, his heart beat harder. He hurried so much that he lost a sandal as he crossed a river. On the day of his arrival, King Pelias was holding games on the seashore. He saw a young man come running toward him with one bare foot. No! This youth was the concrete realization of the oracle. When Jason told King Pelias who he was, Pelias was prepared. He said that Jason must perform a difficult task, and if he did, King Pelias would abdicate the throne to him. The task was complex. A winged ram with Golden Fleece had been sacrificed to

Zeus, and its pelt had been saved. King Pelias demanded that Jason bring him that Golden Fleece.

The Golden Fleece was in the far land of Colchis. It hung from an oak tree and was guarded by a dragon who never slept.

What an adventure! Eager to start, Jason had a ship built with 50 oars. He named it the *Argo* after its builder Argos. The 50 men who sailed it were the Argonauts, the finest sailors in Greece; they included sons of gods and kings. Heracles was among them.

Their first stop was the island of Lemnos. The women there had killed off their men, but they welcomed the Argonauts as fathers for future children. Jason took the

The *Argo* carried Jason and a crew of 50 on the quest for the Golden Fleece. An arduous journey full of danger and intrigue, it ended in betrayal and atrocity.

leader as his wife and fathered twins.

Next they stopped in the land of the Doliones, where they were welcomed. But when they left, stormy winds confused them, and in the night they landed once more among the Doliones, who took them for an enemy that often attacked at night. In the dark the Argonauts killed many, including the king. When daylight came, they lamented their mistake and gave the king a luxurious burial.

The third port was Mysia. One of the men, Hylas, went to draw fresh water. A nymph, excited by his beauty, stole him away. Another man, Polyphemus, heard his cry and thought he'd been robbed. He called Heracles to help him find the youth. Heracles forgot all else and plunged deep into the forest. Finally, the rest of the Argonauts could wait no more; they set sail without them. Hylas was never heard from again. Polyphemus founded the city Cius and became its king. And Heracles went back to his labors, which had been interrupted by this quest.

The fourth port was in the land of the Bebryces. The king there forced strangers to box with him and killed them that way. The Argonaut Polydeuces was a master boxer, however, and he killed the king. The astonished Bebryces attacked. The Argonauts slew many of them as they fled.

The fifth port was Salmydessus, in Thrace. There the Argonauts met the old soothsayer, King Phineas, who had been blinded by the gods for a past offense. The man was tormented by the harpies, two birds with the heads of women. Every time Phineas sat down to eat, the harpies devoured his food and left behind a stench. He begged Jason for help. When food was served and the harpies came, two Argonauts chased them away, never to return again. Then the old man feasted with his guests and gave them advice on how to pass through the Symplegades.

The Symplegades were enormous rocks in the sea that the winds would make crash together. Thick mists cloaked them, and no ship had ever successfully passed between them. But the Argonauts had no choice; Colchis lay on the other side. When the Argo was near the Symplegades, Jason let loose a dove, as Phineas had advised. The dove flew through, losing only a single tail feather. So the *Argo* dared to sail forth. The rocks came smashing through, but they caught only the very

EPIC Voyages

This long voyage, with so many obstacles along the way, is part of a tradition throughout the myths and the epic poems of ancient Greece. We already saw this type of voyage in Heracles' 12 labors. It is carried to the extreme in Homer's tale of Odysseus. It takes Odysseus ten years to return home from the Trojan War; he fights Cyclopes, descends into the Underworld, is tossed by storms, trapped, bewitched. Later the Roman poet Virgil tells a similar tale of Aeneas.

A scene from Homer's tale of Odysseus

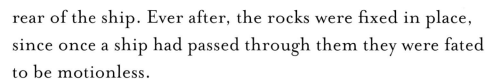

rear of the ship. Ever after, the rocks were fixed in place, since once a ship had passed through them they were fated to be motionless.

Finally, the *Argo* moored in Colchis. Jason went to King Aietes and explained that he needed the Golden Fleece, just like that, as though now everything would fall into place. The king said he would turn it over if Jason yoked the Chalcotaurus bulls without assistance and plowed a field with them, sowing dragon's teeth. These two huge wild bulls had bronze hooves, and they breathed fire. Jason had no idea how to begin.

But Medea did. She was the daughter of the king and a sorceress, and she had fallen in love with this daring stranger. When he pledged his eternal love, she gave him instructions. First, he rubbed himself with a potion that protected him from the bulls' fire. When they charged him, he managed to yoke them and sow the dragon's teeth. Men in armor sprang up from the sown teeth, ready to attack. Jason threw stones in their midst, as Medea had advised, and the soldiers turned upon each other. While they fought, he killed them.

When King Aietes saw that the tasks had been done, he knew Jason couldn't have managed alone. He flew into a rage and threatened to kill the Argonauts. But Medea snuck off with Jason to the oak tree, where they put the dragon to sleep

Jason grabs the Golden Fleece as Medea watches. Without Medea, Jason could not have finished his quest. Her magic let him yoke the ferocious bulls, sow the dragon teeth, drug the dragon guard.

with another magic potion. They took the Golden Fleece back to the *Argo* and the men set off for home, bringing Medea's brother Apsyrtus with them.

King Aietes followed. But Medea chopped her brother up and threw his pieces into the sea. The king stopped to gather the limbs of his slain son, and that delay gave the *Argo* time to get away. But Zeus was furious at what Medea had done to her innocent brother. So he told Jason the *Argo* had to visit the nymph Circe on the island Aeaea, and she would purify them.

They did, and she did, and they continued homeward.

But their troubles were not over. The journey brought them past the three islands of the Sirens. No one had ever seen the Sirens and lived to tell of them. It was rumored that they were mermaids of dazzling beauty and cruel appetites. They sang with voices that bewitched; all who heard naturally turned toward them. Ships then crashed on their islands and the sailors were never heard from again. Jason ordered the Argonaut Orpheus to play his lyre as they drew near, for Orpheus' skill at this instrument rivaled Apollo's. He played loudly and drowned out the Sirens' songs.

The *Argo* managed to skirt past danger after danger, and the quest for the Golden Fleece wound up taking four months.

But King Pelias had no intention of turning over his throne. So Medea called together Pelias' daughters for a

The *Argo* went by the Sirens, who enchanted sailors with their songs and lured them away so they were never seen again. So Orpheus played the lyre loudly, and the Argonauts passed in safety.

demonstration of magic. She cut up an old sheep and threw it into a cauldron with special herbs. The sheep leapt out as a newborn lamb. The daughters were convinced that if they cut up their aging father and boiled him, he'd leap out as a young man again. Instead, of course, Medea didn't add the magical herbs this time, and the girls wound up slaughtering their own father.

Medea and Jason were banished from the country for this deed. They went to Corinth for ten years. Then the king of Corinth offered his daughter Glauce in marriage to Jason, and Jason set aside Medea. How Jason could have thought Medea was a person one could cross is hard to fathom. Medea sent Glauce a robe soaked in poison. When the girl put it on, she was consumed in fire. Then Medea killed the sons she'd had with Jason and fled to Athens where she married King Aegeus.

Many years later, Jason reclaimed the throne of Iolcus, and a later son of his became king there. His own life ended quietly, however. He was asleep under the beached *Argo* when the stern of the old ship broke and fell on him. Some said it was a just ending, since he had broken his promise of eternal love to Medea.

THESEUS The King of Athens

THESEUS
The King of Athens

King Aegeus of Athens was saddened by the fact that he was childless. While traveling through the south of Greece, he stopped in Troezen and met the king's daughter, Aethra, and fell in love. In the morning, he placed a sword and a pair of sandals in a small cavelike hollow, then blocked the entrance with a marble boulder. He told Aethra that if she should have a male child, when the boy was strong enough to move the boulder and fetch the goods beneath it, she should send him to Athens to claim his father.

The child, Theseus, grew faster and stronger than other children, and soon moved the boulder. His grandfather had a ship waiting to take him to Athens. But Theseus chose the more dangerous land route. He loved the tales of the great hero Heracles, who was actually a cousin, and he wanted to prove his own strength and become just as famous a hero.

He did it. The robber Periphetes, who bashed people to death with his club—Theseus smashed his head with that same club and took it for his own. The robber Sinis, who tied people to two pine trees bent to the ground and then released the trees so they flew apart, each taking a section of the poor person tied to them—he was ripped asunder the same way. The robber Sciron, who made his victims kneel to wash his feet and then kicked them into the sea to be eaten by a giant turtle—well, Theseus threw him over a cliff onto the rocks and waves below. The robber Cercyon, who made others wrestle to the death with him—he wrestled to his own death with Theseus. The robber Procrustes, who had two iron beds that he made his victims fit, putting short ones on the long bed and stretching them and putting tall ones on the short bed and cutting off parts—he was likewise fitted to one of his own beds. Each was served with his own crime. This was Theseus' idea of justice— an eye for an eye—and it rang true to the people. They loved him for making the roads safe against robbers. Plus this strapping young fellow had killed a savage sow, as well. What could be better? His reputation preceded him to Athens.

King Aegeus had no idea that the famed young stranger named Theseus was his son. But he feared that the youth was becoming so popular the people might overthrow him and make Theseus king. His wife at the time, a magician called Medea, who had once been married to Jason, proposed to poison Theseus. At the banquet in honor of the young hero, Medea handed him the poisoned cup. But Theseus, in his eagerness to be united with his father, drew his sword.

GREAT Thinkers

Theseus fighting the Minotaur

Theseus, like Heracles, was a famous hero, but of a very different type. Brave and strong, he was also a thinker. He solved problems via intellect and compassion. Theseus ruled Athens, the birthplace of democracy and some of the world's greatest thinkers. Socrates is known for ethics. Plato is known for logic and mathematics. Aeschylus and Sophocles wrote tragic plays. Euripides' plays gave voice to the intelligence of women, slaves, and powerless people. Modern thought owes much to ancient Athens.

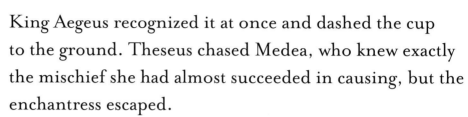

King Aegeus recognized it at once and dashed the cup to the ground. Theseus chased Medea, who knew exactly the mischief she had almost succeeded in causing, but the enchantress escaped.

The king now proclaimed Theseus as his heir, and the young man immediately saw an opportunity to gain the love of the Athenians. Many years before, King Minos of Crete had sent his only son to Athens for a visit. King Aegeus had made the terrible mistake of sending the boy to kill a bull; but the bull killed the boy. Crazed with grief, Minos invaded Athens and threatened to burn it to the ground unless seven maidens and seven youths were sent to him once every nine years. The 14 young people were to be given to the Minotaur.

The Minotaur was the most unfortunate of beasts. Long ago the god Poseidon had given Minos a bull to be sacrificed to Poseidon himself. The bull was magnificent, and Minos couldn't bear to kill it, so he kept it. Angered, Poseidon made Minos' wife, Pasiphaë, fall in love with it. From their

Theseus entered the Labyrinth and managed to find his way out again, thanks to the wiles of Ariadne, who advised him to carry thread and unwind it to mark his path.

union came the Minotaur, a man with a bull head. Like the hybrid centaurs, the Minotaur was flesh-hungry. The 14 young Athenians were to be his meal.

Theseus arrived in Athens just days before the next group of 14 young people were to be carried off to Crete in a ship with the black sails of misery. He offered to go in place of one of the youths. As the boat took off, Theseus told his father he would kill the Minotaur and come home with white sails of joy.

The Minotaur lived in the Labyrinth, a structure built especially for him, with paths that led in circles, so that no one could ever escape. As the Athenian youths were paraded through the streets on their way to this most terrifying doom, the people of Crete watched in a mix of horror and gratitude that the children of others were being sacrificed instead of their own. The king's daughter, Ariadne, spied Theseus from her balcony and fell in love. She had him brought to her and said she'd tell him the way to escape, if he'd then marry her. Theseus agreed, and Ariadne gave him a ball of thread. He was to tie one end to the entrance

door of the Labyrinth, then unwind as he walked. That way he could retrace his steps. She had learned this trick from Daedalus, the architect of the Labyrinth.

Theseus walked on careful feet, climbing over rocks silent as a goat kid. He found the Minotaur asleep, his head heavy with two thick horns, resting on his chest. As Theseus crept closer, the stench of the massive beast's blood breath made his own blood race. It was kill or be devoured. Theseus beat him with his bare fists. The beast woke, eyes full of tragedy. Theseus beat with the speed of a hummingbird's wings but the heft of wild horse hooves. He beat even when his fists were bloody stumps. He beat even when it was clear nothing moved but his fists— nothing else lived. The pitiable creature died dazed.

Theseus followed the thread trail back to the Labyrinth door, leading the other Athenian youths. He found Ariadne and they all got in the ship and headed back toward Athens, stopping at Naxos, an island sacred to the god Dionysus. There Theseus had one of the least fine moments of his life. He looked at Ariadne, asleep on the beach, and realized he didn't want a wife right now, or, at least not this wife. So he set sail, abandoning her there in her sleep. Fortunately for the girl, she and Dionysus got along well, and they married. In his rush home, Theseus forgot to change the black sails to white. King Aegeus saw the sails and imagined the Minotaur's mouth dripping with the blood of his

Theseus beat the Minotaur to death with his bare fists, rather than using a rock or a knife. Perhaps the savagery of the monster ignited his own bestial side.

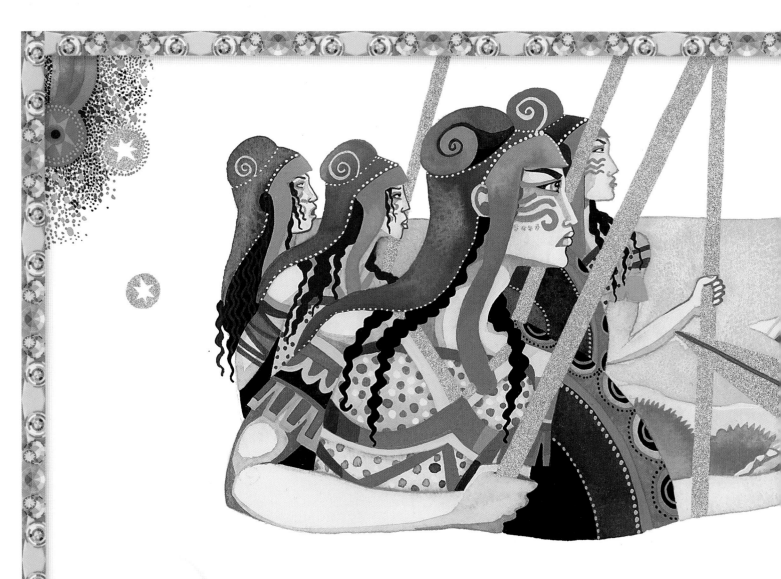

Theseus and his cousin Heracles fought the Amazons, killing many. But Theseus married the pretty Amazon princess Antiope and brought her back to Athens.

son. He threw himself from a cliff and died.

The bereaved Theseus became king of Athens. But he didn't savor power. Instead, he gathered the people together and told them to vote for what they wanted. He created the first democracy of the known world. And he behaved with a new wisdom, quite different from the behavior he had shown as a young man when he had disposed of the robbers. When the city of Thebes had a war with the Argives and refused to bury the dead Argive soldiers, Theseus marched against them. He conquered Thebes and made the Thebans bury the dead, but then he left, without harming Thebes at all. When his cousin Heracles went mad and killed his family, Theseus stood by him and said wrong done in a maddened state was not evil, and

Heracles should not kill himself, but should seek a source of peace. No more eye-for-an-eye justice; Theseus had learned humanity.

Never did he give up his love of danger, though. He accompanied Heracles to fight the infamous women warriors known as Amazons and took one for his wife. He joined King Pirithous to fight the centaurs after they had gotten drunk at a wedding and assaulted the bride. He became infatuated with a very young but very beautiful maiden from Sparta named Helen, and kidnapped her, knowing full well that the Spartans were the most vicious army on Earth. He intended to marry her, but while he was off in Tartarus on another adventure, the Spartans invaded Athens and took Helen back.

Like Heracles, the hero Theseus met a terrible end. Somehow he lost favor with the Athenians and was driven away to the land of Scyros, where the king, Lycomede, threw him to his death in an abyss.

HELEN
The Lethal Beauty

King Peleus of Phthia married the nymph goddess Thetis, whose feet slipped over land like silver moonglow. They invited gods and goddesses to their wedding—all but one, Eris, the goddess of discord, because she was known for ruining everything. Eris smarted. She determined to ruin the wedding anyway. She threw an apple into the midst of the guests with the label "for the fairest." All the goddesses wanted it, naturally. But in the end none but the three most powerful put themselves forward: Hera, Athena, and Aphrodite. They asked Zeus to choose. Only an idiot would have accepted the task. Zeus immediately thought of Paris, the prince of the distant city of Troy. The prince's mother, Hecuba, had had a terrible dream, which his father, King Priam, interpreted in the worst way: The dream meant his son would one day bring fiery ruin to the country. So King Priam had sent Paris to Mount Ida to keep sheep and stay out of trouble. The exiled prince married the nymph Oenone and seemed happy. Paris was a dimwit, as far as Zeus could see. He was the perfect idiot for this task. Zeus told the three goddesses to go ask Paris.

The goddesses were callous about it; beauty wasn't an objective matter anyway. They offered bribes. Hera offered political power: Paris could become leader of Europe and Asia. Athena offered military power: Paris could lead the Trojans in war against Greece and win. Aphrodite offered love power: Paris could marry the most beautiful human woman. Paris chose Aphrodite and went off to claim his wife, with never a backward glance at the poor nymph Oenone.

Who was the most beautiful human woman? A daughter of Zeus, of course. Leda, the wife of King Tyndareus of Sparta, had the whitest arms, legs, neck. Her eyes were black pitch, her mouth red blood, her tongue the color of pomegranate juice. She moved as though gliding on water, peaceful, aloof. A perfect target. Zeus came in the form he thought befit her, a huge white swan. In a single night four children began growing inside Leda: the boy Castor and the girl Clytemnestra, children of her husband Tyndareus, and the boy Polydeuces and the girl Helen, children of Zeus.

By the time Helen was ten, word of her beauty had spread. She had the grace of her mother, but something else, too, something more profoundly moving. She made men feel like their bones had turned to water. By the time she was twelve, suitors came. The great Theseus even stole her away, only to

Helen looking down

FEMMES Fatales

Mythical women of intoxicating beauty come up in many cultures. Celtic lore had Queen Maeve. Hindu lore had enchanting Mohini. And the ancient Greeks had Aphrodite and Helen. Often these beauties have admirable strengths: Queen Maeve was a powerful warrior. But often these beauties lead men into bad situations; such a beauty is called a "femme fatale." For love of Helen, war was waged for ten years, with many warriors slaughtered on both sides. Helen might be the most "fatale" of "femmes."

have her be stolen back by her brothers. King Tyndareus was afraid fights might break out if he chose among the throngs of suitors, so he made the men promise to support whoever became Helen's husband. Then Tyndareus chose Menelaus, brother to King Agamemnon of Mycenae. King Tyndareus abdicated the throne and Menelaus became king of Sparta. Helen bore him a daughter, Hermione. Motherhood only served to make her eyes appear deeper, her cheeks fuller—she was altogether more beautiful.

Paris, prince of Troy, set off to claim Helen. He arrived in Sparta with many ships. King Menelaus entertained him graciously, unaware of the prince's intentions. On the tenth day of his visit, the king left for a funeral in Crete, and Paris convinced Helen to flee with him that night, abandoning her family.

Menelaus turned to Helen's past suitors for support. That included nearly all the powerful men of Greece. They had promised Tyndareus; it was time to keep that promise. A thousand ships prepared to set sail eastward.

But the winds wouldn't blow; the ships sat idle. King

When the Trojan prince Paris stole the Greek queen Helen, ships carrying Greek soldiers crossed the Aegean Sea to wage war on Troy. Ten years of death and misery ensued.

Agamemnon of Mycenae—brother of Menelaus, husband of Helen's sister Clytemnestra—was commander of the whole force. He made the incredibly stupid and tragic mistake of killing a stag and boasting he was a better hunter than the goddess Artemis. It was Artemis who kept the winds from blowing. She demanded that Agamemnon sacrifice the first girl he saw before she'd let the boats sail. Agamemnon's chariot turned the bend, and there was his sweet daughter, Iphigenia, niece of Helen. Distraught, the trapped king had his daughter beheaded, a hideous task.

The winds howled and the ships sailed. A youth, but 15 years old, the son of King Peleus and the nymph Thetis, whose wedding had started this whole affair—this youth was in charge of the fleet. His name was Achilles. His mother had dipped the boy as an infant in the River Styx in Tartarus to make him immortal. But she held him by one heel, and that heel remained his point of vulnerability. When the war was declared, Thetis, convinced he'd die in battle, had dressed Achilles as a girl and sent him to another court for safety.

But the soldier Odysseus laid a trap for the disguised Achilles. He went to the court and showed the women beautiful jewels and sharp daggers. One girl cared nothing for the jewels but spent all her time looking at the daggers—and so Odysseus hauled the young Achilles off to war.

Over in Troy, thousands of young men assembled to fight for their country's honor. King Priam's son Hector, brother of Paris, was the greatest Trojan warrior. Unlike Paris, Hector was trustworthy and thoughtful. He knew, just as the Greek Achilles knew, that this war meant certain death, yet he took up his arms with courage.

See them? See these fine young people, armed to the teeth, hearts full of valor and hope, but heads knowing rivers of blood would flow. See them battle month after month, year after year—egged on by gods and goddesses who saw them as pawns in a giant game. See their sense of loyalty tested. See their knowledge of honor develop. Cry for them. Cry for soldiers everywhere. Cry for their families. Cry for the world.

The god Apollo, egotistical to the point of mania, refused to let the war end. For nine years one side was winning, then the other. Achilles killed the dear and true Hector and dragged his body through the mud, for war can make one crazy. Then Paris killed the great warrior Achilles. Both sides had lost really. But they kept fighting, mindlessly, numbly.

In the tenth year, a prophet said Troy could not be taken without the bow and arrows of Heracles. Heracles had already died, burned on a pyre of his own making. But he had given his bow and arrows to his friend Philoctetes. Philoctetes had set out for Troy ten years before, but when his ship stopped at the island of Lemnos, a sea serpent had bitten him. Everyone knew a sea serpent's bite was fatal; the ship abandoned Philoctetes. Now Odysseus led a party back to Lemnos to look for the bow and arrows. Amazingly, they found Philoctetes still alive. They brought him back to Troy, and Philoctetes killed Paris with an arrow.

But the war still didn't end, for Helen was hidden somewhere

Warriors gathered, shields and swords ready. The youth of two nations fought out of honor and loyalty but, sadly, in a battle that served more to amuse the gods than anything else.

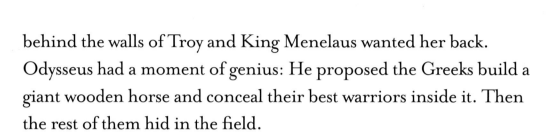

behind the walls of Troy and King Menelaus wanted her back. Odysseus had a moment of genius: He proposed the Greeks build a giant wooden horse and conceal their best warriors inside it. Then the rest of them hid in the field.

When the Trojans saw the horse alone on the battlefield, they thought the Greeks had fled, leaving a gift of appeasement. They opened the city gates and pulled the horse inside. Cassandra—sister of dead Hector and dead Paris, daughter of King Priam and Queen Hecuba—warned that the horse was full of warriors who would destroy Troy. No one believed her. That was her gift, to see the future. That was her curse, never to be believed.

Helen looked at the horse warily. She walked around it, calling out the soldiers' names using the voices of their wives. Within the horse, the Greek soldiers squirmed; they were almost tricked. But Odysseus made them all stay quiet. And Helen went to sleep, having assured herself that Cassandra was wrong.

As the Trojans slept, the Greeks climbed out. They opened the city gates so that the armies waiting outside could come in. The Greek soldiers slaughtered the Trojan soldiers in their beds as they slept. Menelaus found Helen and took her to his ship. The Greeks burned the city to the ground and left.

Helen grieved for the slaughter she had caused by giving in to Paris' seduction. But all of it—from Helen's luminous beauty to the interminable war—was the doing of gods with too much time on their hands.

The Greeks built a giant horse and hid inside. The Trojans accepted the "gift" and rolled it within their walls. And so the war finally ended, with a brilliant hoax.

This map shows the locations of the ancient sites mentioned in the book.

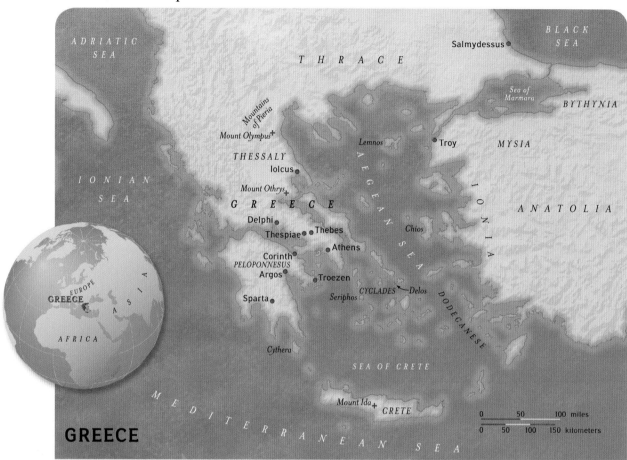

GREECE

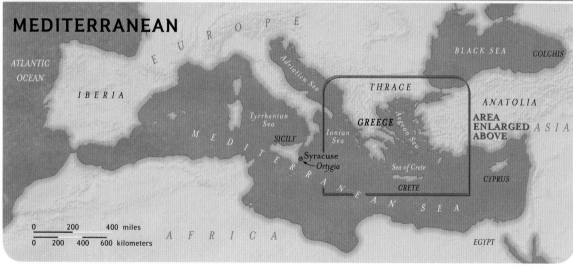

MEDITERRANEAN

TIME LINE

1900 B.C.
Indo-European tribes known as Mycenaeans overrun Greece and introduce their language. Ancient Greek (the language our myths were originally written in) gradually forms around this time.

1400 B.C.
The Mycenaeans extend their control to the island of Crete. Athens becomes an important trade center.

1100 B.C.-800 B.C.
The Mycenaean civilization is gradually overcome and replaced by the civilization that embraces the mythology presented in this book. City-states (that is, cities with walls around them that had their own governments) arise.

800 B.C. (roughly)
The Greek alphabet is formed. From this point on, most major works in Greece are written in the Greek alphabet.

750-650 B.C.
The ancient Greek poets Hesiod and Homer write the stories that give us our first information about Greek mythology. Hesiod's *Theogony* tells about the origins of the world and of the gods. Homer's *Iliad* tells about the Trojan War and his *Odyssey* tells about the travels of Odysseus as he returns from Troy to Greece.

550 B.C.
Athens is widely recognized as the cultural center of Greece. Greece, particularly Athens, becomes a center for dramatic theater for the next 300 years.

525-455 B.C.
The playwright Aeschylus lives. He writes tragedies that are still studied and performed today. His play *The Oresteia,* is about the curse on the house of the King Atreus.

497-406 B.C.
The playwright Sophocles lives. He writes tragedies, also well-known today. One of his most famous is called *Oedipus,* about a young man who falls in love with his mother.

480-406 B.C.
The playwright Euripides lives. He writes tragedies that are unusual in that the women characters play prominent, strong roles, slaves are often presented as intelligent, and gods and heroes are often laughed at.

469-399 B.C.
The philosopher Socrates lives. His writings lay the foundation for Western philosophy.

428-348 B.C.
Plato, a student of Socrates, lives. His written dialogues become central to philosophy, language, mathematics, logic, and ethics.

29-19 B.C.
The Roman poet Virgil writes *The Aeneid,* the story of the travels of the Trojan soldier Aeneas after the Trojan War. Aeneas is the mythological ancestor of the ancient Romans.

0 B.C./A.D. (roughly)
In the years before and after the year zero, the Roman poet Ovid produces works that give us much information about native Roman mythology as well as Roman mythology imported from Greece.

CAST OF CHARACTERS

GODS & GODDESSES

Name: APHRODITE
Roman Name: Venus
Title: Goddess of Love & Beauty
Generation: Olympian
Symbols: scallop shell, myrtle, dove, sparrow, girdle, mirror, swan
Birthplace: in the sea, near Cyprus
Married to: Hephaestus
Parents: Uranus

Greek Name: ARTEMIS
Roman Name: Diana
Title: Goddess of the Hunt
Generation: Olympian
Symbols: bow and arrow, deer, wild goat, boar, quail
Birthplace: Ortygia
Parents: Zeus and Leto

Greek Name: APOLLO
Roman Name: Apollo
Title: God of Music
Generation: Olympian
Symbols: lyre, crown of laurel, hawk, raven, fawn
Birthplace: Delos
Parents: Zeus and Leto

Greek Name: ATHENA
Roman Name: Minerva
Title: Goddess of Wisdom
Generation: Olympian
Symbols: olive tree, aegis, owl, snake, distaff
Birthplace: unknown
Parents: Zeus and Metis

Greek Name: ARES
Roman Name: Mars
Title: God of War
Generation: Olympian
Symbols: spear and sword
Birthplace: unknown
Parents: Zeus and Hera

Greek Name: CRONUS
Roman Name: Saturn
Title: Titan King
Generation: Titan
Symbol: none
Birthplace: from Gaia
Married to: Rhea
Parents: Uranus and Gaia

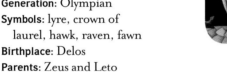

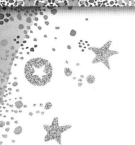

Greek Name: DEMETER
Roman Name: Ceres
Title: Goddess of the Harvest
Generation: Olympian
Symbols: wheat sheaf, torch, sacrificial bowl
Birthplace: unknown
Parents: Cronus and Rhea

Greek Name: HADES
Roman Name: Pluto
Title: God of the Underworld
Generation: Olympian
Symbol: cap of darkness, chariot and horses, scepter
Birthplace: unknown
Married to: Persephone
Parents: Cronus and Rhea

Greek Name: DIONYSUS
Roman Name: Bacchus
Title: God of Wine
Generation: Olympian
Symbol: grape vines, bull, ivy
Birthplace: unknown
Married to: many wives
Parents: Zeus and Semele

Greek Name: HELIOS
Roman Name: Sol
Title: Sun God
Generation: Titan
Symbol: chariot
Birthplace: unknown
Parents: Hyperion and Theia

Greek Name: GAIA
Roman Name: Gaia
Title: Mother Earth
Generation: Primordial
Symbol: cow
Birthplace: the void
Married to: Uranus
Parents: appeared out of Chaos

Greek Name: HEPHAESTUS
Roman Name: Vulcan
Title: God of Metalworking
Generation: Olympian
Symbol: fire, hammer, anvil, forge, bellows
Birthplace: unknown
Married to: Aphrodite
Parents: Hera

GODS & GODDESSES (CONTINUED)

Greek Name: HERA
Roman Name: Juno
Title: Goddess of Marriage
Generation: Olympian
Symbol: peacocks,
    wedding veil, cuckoo
Birthplace: unknown
Married to: Zeus
Parents: Cronus and Rhea

Greek Name: SELENE
Roman Name: Luna
Title: Goddess of the Moon
Generation: Titan
Symbols: silver chariot,
    crescent moon
Birthplace: the sky
Married to: Endymion
Parents: Hyperion and Theia

Greek Name: HERMES
Roman Name: Mercury
Title: Messenger of the Gods
Generation: Olympian
Symbol: winged sandals,
    broad-brimmed hat, ram,
    tortoiseshell lyre
Birthplace: Cyllene cave
Parents: Zeus and Maia

Greek Name: URANUS
Roman Name: Uranus
Title: Father Heaven
Generation: Primordial
Symbol: none
Birthplace: everywhere; he
    appeared before there were
    fixed places in the world
Married to: Gaia
Parents: Gaia

Greek Name: HESTIA
Roman Name: Vesta
Title: Goddess of the Hearth
Generation: Olympian
Symbol: the hearth
Birthplace: unknown
Parents: Cronus and Rhea

Greek Name: ZEUS
Roman Name: Jupiter
Title: King of the Gods
Generation: Olympian
Symbol: thunderbolt, scepter,
    scales, aegis, eagle, lion, throne
Birthplace: Olympus
Married to: Hera was his queen,
    but he married many goddesses
    and mortals
Parents: Cronus and Rhea

Greek Name: POSEIDON
Roman Name: Neptune
Title: God of the Seas
Generation: Olympian
Symbol: trident, horse, bull
Birthplace: unknown
Married to: Medusa, then Euryale
Parents: Cronus and Rhea

HEROES & MORTALS

Greek Name: HELEN
Title: The Lethal Beauty
Birthplace: Sparta
Married to: Menelaus
Parents: Zeus and Leda

Greek Name: PERSEUS
Title: The Ill-fated Hero
Birthplace: Argos
Married to: Andromeda
Parents: Zeus and Danaë

Greek Name: HERACLES
Roman Name: Hercules
Title: The Hero Who
Became Immortal
Birthplace: Troezen
Married to: Megara, then
Deianeira
Parents: Zeus and Alcmene

Greek Name: THESEUS
Title: The King of Athens
Birthplace: Troezen
Married to: Ariadne, then an
Amazon wife
Parents: Aegeus and Aethra

Greek Name: JASON
Title: Wanderer of the Seas
Birthplace: Iolcus
Married to: Medea, then Clauce
Parents: Aeson and Alcimede

Greek Name: ORION
Title: The Hunter
Birthplace: unknown
Married to: unmarried
Parents: Poseidon and Euryale

BIBLIOGRAPHIC NOTE

The major sources influencing the stories here are the poems of the ancient Greek named Hesiod, and the poems and hymns of his contemporary, Homer. R. M. Frazer's translation, *The Poems of Hesiod*, includes *Theogony* and *Works and Days,* with helpful comments. Apostolos N. Athanassakis's translation, *The Homeric Hymns,* also has wonderful notes. If neither Hesiod nor Homer wrote about a particular mythological event I wanted to handle, I turned next to the *Library of Greek Mythology* by scholar Apollodorus, who lived in the second century B.C. Robin Hard's translation and notes for this great work were invaluable. At times I also turned to the works of the Roman poet Ovid, mostly for the beauty of the language. Two translations of the poem *Metamorphoses,* as well as the original, influenced me most: those of Charles Martin, in poetry, and of Michael Simpson, in prose. And when choosing which tales to include, I often went back to the book I've owned and loved since I took my first Latin course in ninth grade, that of Edith Hamilton. Whenever other sources disagreed with Hesiod and Homer, the ancient Greeks won, since this book is a treasury of Greek mythology. Whenever Hesiod and Homer disagreed with each other, Hesiod won, because his *Theogony,* in particular, felt so authoritative to me.

Checking my work, feeding me resources, offering advice and encouragement at every step of the way was my dear friend Rosaria Munson, to whom I am forever grateful.

Apollodorus. 1997. *The Library of Greek Mythology.* Translated with an introduction and notes by Robin Hard. Oxford: Oxford University Press.

Athanassakis, Apostolos N. 1976. *The Homeric Hymns.* Baltimore, MD: Johns Hopkins University Press.

Frazer, R. M. 1983. *The Poems of Hesiod.* Norman, OK: University of Oklahoma Press.

Hamilton, Edith. 1940. *Mythology.* New York: The New American Library of World Literature, Inc.

Ovid. 2004. *Metamorphoses.* Translated and with notes by Charles Martin. New York: W.W. Norton & Company.

Simpson, Michael. 2001. *The Metamorphoses of Ovid.* Amherst, MA: University of Massachusetts Press.

FIND OUT MORE

BOOKS

Amery, Heather. *Greek Myths for Young Children.* London: Usborne, 1999.

Coats, Lucy, and Anthony Lewis. *Atticus the Storyteller's 100 Greek Myths.* London: Orion, 2003.

D'Aulaire, Ingri, and Edgar Parin. *The D'Aulaires' Book of Greek Myths.* New York: Random House, 1992.

Roberts, Jennifer T., and Tracy Barrett. *The Ancient Greek World.* Oxford: Oxford University Press, 2004.

Sutcliff, Rosemary. *Black Ships Before Troy: The Story of the Iliad.* London: Laurel Leaf, 2005.

——. *The Wanderings of Odysseus: The Story of The Odyssey.* London: Laurel Leaf, 2002.

TELEVISION

Jim Henson's The Storyteller: Greek Myths. Television series available on DVD, written and directed by Anthony Minghella. The Jim Henson Company, 1987.

WEB SITES

Starfall's I'm Reading: Greek Myths. http://www.starfall.com/n/level-c/index/play.htm?f.

Mythological map of Greece. http://www.sigmabooks.gr/maps_en_enGreece.html.

Mythweb Encyclopedia Mythica. http://www.mythweb.com.

Greek Mythology Link. http://www.maicar.com/GML.

INDEX

Illustrations are indicated by **boldface**. If illustrations are included within a page span, the entire span is **boldface**.

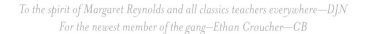

To the spirit of Margaret Reynolds and all classics teachers everywhere—DJN
For the newest member of the gang—Ethan Croucher—CB

Published by the National Geographic Society
John M. Fahey, Jr., *Chairman of the Board and Chief Executive Officer*
Timothy T. Kelly, *President*
Declan Moore, *Executive Vice President; President, Publishing*
Melina Gerosa Bellows, *Executive Vice President; Chief Creative Officer,*
Books, Kids, and Family

Prepared by the Book Division
Nancy Laties Feresten, *Senior Vice President, Editor in Chief, Children's Books*
Jonathan Halling, *Design Director, Books and Children's Publishing*
Jay Sumner, *Director of Photography, Children's Publishing*
Jennifer Emmett, *Editorial Director, Children's Books*
Carl Mehler, *Director of Maps*
R. Gary Colbert, *Production Director*
Jennifer A. Thornton, *Managing Editor*

Staff for This Book
Priyanka Lamichhane, *Project Editor*
David M. Seager, *Art Director/Designer*
Lori Epstein, *Senior Illustrations Editor*
Kate Olesin, *Editorial Assistant*
Kathryn Robbins, *Design Production Assistant*
Hillary Moloney, *Illustrations Assistant*
Grace Hill, *Associate Managing Editor*
Gregory Ugiansky, *Map Research and Production*
Joan Gossett, *Production Editor*
Lewis R. Bassford, *Production Manager*
Susan Borke, *Legal and Business Affairs*

Manufacturing and Quality Management
Christopher A. Liedel, *Chief Financial Officer*
Phillip L. Schlosser, *Senior Vice President*
Chris Brown, *Technical Director*
Nicole Elliott, *Manager*
Rachel Faulise, *Manager*
Robert L. Barr, *Manager*

The National Geographic Society is one of the world's largest nonprofit scientific and educational organizations. Founded in 1888 to "increase and diffuse geographic knowledge," the Society works to inspire people to care about the planet. National Geographic reflects the world through its magazines, television programs, films, music and radio, books, DVDs, maps, exhibitions, live events, school publishing programs, interactive media and merchandise. *National Geographic* magazine, the Society's official journal, published in English and 33 local-language editions, is read by more than 38 million people each month. The National Geographic Channel reaches 320 million households in 34 languages in 166 countries. National Geographic Digital Media receives more than 15 million visitors a month. National Geographic has funded more than 9,400 scientific research, conservation and exploration projects and supports an education program promoting geography literacy.
For more information, visit nationalgeographic.com.

For more information, please call 1-800-NGS LINE (647-5463) or write to the following address:

National Geographic Society
1145 17th Street N.W.
Washington, D.C. 20036-4688 U.S.A.

Visit us online at www.nationalgeographic.com/books
For librarians and teachers: www.ngchildrensbooks.org
More for kids from National Geographic: kids.nationalgeographic.com
For information about special discounts for bulk purchases, please contact National Geographic Books Special Sales: ngspecsales@ngs.org
For rights or permissions inquiries, please contact National Geographic Books Subsidiary Rights: ngbookrights@ngs.org

Text copyright © 2011 Donna Jo Napoli
Illustrations copyright © 2011 Christina Balit
Compilation copyright © 2011 National Geographic Society

National Geographic Society would like to thank Rosaria Munson, professor of classics at Swarthmore College, for her thoughtful review throughout the process of creating this book. In addition, the Society would like to thank Deborah Roberts, professor of classics and comparative literature at Haverford College, for her generous assistance with resources for this title. The publisher gratefully acknowledges Frances Lincoln, Ltd., for their kindness in licensing several previously published pieces of artwork by Christina Balit.

Library of Congress Cataloging-in-Publication Data
Napoli, Donna Jo, 1948-
Treasury of Greek mythology : classic stories of gods, goddesses, heroes & monsters / by Donna Jo Napoli ; illustrated by Christina Balit.
p. cm.
Includes bibliographical references and index.
ISBN 978-1-4263-0844-4 (hardcover : alk. paper) -- ISBN 978-1-4263-0845-1 (library binding : alk. paper)
1. Mythology, Greek--Juvenile literature. I. Balit, Christina. II. Title.
BL783.N365 2011
398.20938--dc23
2011024327

Photo Credits
All artwork by Christina Balit unless otherwise noted below:
15, keren-seg/ Shutterstock; 19, Byron W.Moore/ Shutterstock; 25, jaimaa/ Shutterstock; 31, stoyanh/ Shutterstock; 32-33, Christina Balit; 37, Araldo de Luca/ Corbis; 43, Murat Taner/ Getty Images; 49, Photolibrary.com; 55, Erich Lessing/ Art Resource, NY; 61, Hunor Focze/ Shutterstock; 67, Arte & Immagini srl/ Corbis; 75, Stapleton Collection/ Corbis; 81, Jose AS Reyes/ Shutterstock; 85, The Bridgeman Art Library/ Getty Images; 91, Kevin Carden/ Shutterstock; 97, PoodlesRock/ Corbis; 103, Sandro Vannini/ Corbis; 109, Igor Kovalchuk/ Shutterstock; 115, NASA; 121, Christopher Boswell/ Shutterstock; 127, Bettmann/ Corbis; 137, David Aguilar; 143, Danilo Ascione/ Shutterstock; 155, Erich Lessing/ Art Resource, NY; 163, Bettmann/ Corbis; 173, Mimmo Jodice/ Corbis

Printed in the United States of America
14/RRDW-CML/7 (Hardcover)